HOW I
GOT HIM
TO
MARRY ME
50 TRUE STORIES

CHERISE KELLEY

DEDICATION

To Scott:
You're my light
after all the other lights have gone out.

AUTHOR'S NOTE

I am writing novels based on some of these
50 true Marry Me stories.
Be notified when these novels come out!
Sign up here:
http://eepurl.com/w96_v

CONTENTS

INTRODUCTION

Living together instead of getting married began to be acceptable in the 1960s hippie culture, and by the 1980s, many young men no longer saw the point in marriage. I watched the culture change, but I didn't catch on until it was almost too late for me. Before the 1980s, the man was the one who pushed for marriage. By the 1990s, living together instead of being married was almost expected among young people. Now, in the 21st century, women have a hard time getting married, even if we really want to. If you've been under a rock and haven't noticed this, then search the Internet for the page titled "US Census Marriage and Divorce," and prepare to have your mind blown.

In writing this book, I asked 50 women who got married after 1990:

"How did you get him to marry you, and not just live together?"

I got 50 great responses, and as an added bonus, most of the women explain how they met their future husbands, too. I'll share my own answer first.

I didn't get married until I was 31. I had been engaged twice before that. The first time I was only 17, so I don't really count that one. The second time I was engaged I was 19, and the year was 1982. Both of these guys begged me to marry them! They were way more into marriage than I was. Silly me, I let them both get away.

Getting a groom would always be this easy, right?

Little did I know.

I was 23 when I was finally ready to get married. By then, the year was 1986, and none of the guys I knew wanted to tie the knot! One who I wanted to marry said:

"Children are the only reason I can see to get married, and I don't want any of those."

Saddened, I slowly let go of him and moved on. After that, I guess I was getting long in the tooth. By the time I was in my late 20s, men were no longer begging me to marry them. The stakes had decreased considerably.

In 1989, a guy pursued me urgently, sending roses even. Expecting a proposal, I asked him what he wanted, and he told me:

"I want to buy a house with you."

"Oh." (Is that all? That's not very appealing!)

In 1990, a man who was a bit of a player had the chance to propose, and said:

"I want you to be my one and only girlfriend."

Nuh Uh.

I finally did get married in 1994, and like I said, I was 31 years old. It took me eight years to find him, once I made up my mind that I wanted a husband and not just another boyfriend. For me, that's what it took: I just needed to stick to the decision that I was not going to have another boyfriend. I was only going to have a husband.

Scott and I met at the airport. It was December, but I was coming from Los Angeles where it was warm, so I only had on shorts and a T shirt. I was cold. I looked around for someone wearing a coat that I could borrow for a few minutes, just to warm up. I saw Scott sitting there wearing a down parka that we've kept these 20 years.

"Hi."

"Hi."

"Could I borrow your coat for a minute, just to warm up?"

"Sure."

Wouldn't you know, it turned out we were on the same flight. He switched seats so he could sit next to me and get his coat back. He was stationed 1,000 miles away, in the US Navy, coming home on leave to see his parents. He asked me out, but I explained I had a boyfriend. He asked if I would be his pen pal, and that I agreed to, you know, just to support the troops.

Over the next year, we wrote back and forth often. After my boyfriend dumped me on my 30th birthday, Scott and I started talking on the phone every evening, for hours. This was 1993, when you still paid long distance charges. We each paid a $500 phone bill every month! Whenever he came home on leave, we would go out.

When he asked me to be his girlfriend, I surprised him by saying, "No." We were on the phone, as we were every night. I could tell he was hurt, but since we were on the phone and not together in person, we had to talk, and that was a good thing.

I explained, "I'm 30 years old. I've already had the last boyfriend I am ever going to have. In the future, I am going to have a husband, not a boyfriend."

He surprised me by taking this in stride. "I understand," he said. "You do realize I am in the Navy and all that entails?"

"I was born in the Navy!" This was true. My dad was in the Navy.

Four months later, he took me on a date to the top of the Space Needle in Seattle.

He passed me a little black velvet box under the table, and whispered:

"Babe, will you marry me?"

"Do you mean it?"

That's what I said. Not very romantic, was I?

* * *

Because this book may be of interest to cultural anthropologists such as Alan Dundes, my folklore professor at UC Berkeley, I'd like to discuss the methodology I used to collect these stories, and two trends I noticed in these 50 women's responses to the question of how they got their men to marry them and not just live together for the rest of their lives.

Many of the men in the stories say dismissive things about marriage and make excuses for not committing to their women, such as:

"If it ain't broke, don't fix it,"

and,

"Marriage is just a piece of paper."

Many of the women compare marriage to a fairy tale where everyone lives "happily ever after."

I understand both sides.

Like many of the reluctant grooms in these stories, I come from a broken home. When I was 9 and my sister was 5, our parents yelled at each other across the house constantly. They never physically hurt each other, but they did do damage. Less than a year later, my parents were divorced.

Like many of the yearning brides in these stories,

as a young girl I loved fairy tales, weddings, and fancy dresses. I didn't connect these three things until I collected these stories. In her fantasies, every little girl is a fairy-tale princess: someone who wears fancy dresses and dances with a charming and attentive prince. Like most brides and grooms, Scott and I danced together at our wedding dressed as Prince Charming and his princess. My parents put aside their differences and danced together there, too. It was like magic.

I collected (and paid for exclusive rights to) these 50 "How I Got Him to Marry Me" stories January 26 - February 28, 2013 through an online questionnaire on an article-writing website. Each respondent only saw the questionnaire. She did not see the other responses.

On the next page is the questionnaire, which was posed as a paid writing assignment and went through a few changes over the course of the month it was posted.

For those of you who got married after the year 1990: How did you convince him to marry you and not just live together?

For your story to be accepted, you must:

1) Write your true heterosexual story from the woman's point of view, in first person ("I"), about getting married after the year 1990. Write a story, not an article. Stay with the story. Do not reference any sources. Get right to the story. Do not write any introduction. Do not repeat yourself. Each sentence must add new information to the story. Write in whichever form of English is most natural for you. Write as if you are telling a friend, "I said _____, and then he said, _____." Your tone should be conversational and engaging. Maybe playful if your story is funny.

2) Rated G. Nothing sexual. You can politely tell about how you refrained from having sex until and unless you were married, but otherwise avoid any sexual topics. No stories about getting pregnant in order to force him to marry you. (We all know that doesn't work anymore!) No stories about him divorcing her to marry you. [About mid way through the project, I added here, "You must still be happily married." I had received 3 stories which were too sad to include in this anthology.]

3) There must be something interesting about your story. It cannot be boring, vague, or ordinary. Give details. Get into the who, what, when, where, why and how.

Examples: Quote what the two of you said if your conversations were juicy. Explain where you got your ideas if they were surprising. Tell about the event that changed his mind, if that's what happened.

4) Your story must answer questions a-d below, but do not include these questions in your submission. You do not have to go in this order.

a) What objections did he have to getting married? (There must be at least one objection.)

b) What did you say or do to overcome these objections?

c) What year were you married?

d) How did you get him to marry you, rather than just live together?

5) Include your first name and his first name. Fake names are OK so long as they sound real. The names you provide may be published, but you agree that I am buying exclusive rights to this story and I can publish it under whatever name I wish. You may not post or publish this story anywhere else. You release all rights to it. [I left the names alone and published them as they were given to me.]

6) Each author can only contribute one assignment to this project. You might see other assignments with similar titles and descriptions, but you can only do one.

I edited the stories to make them easier to read and more entertaining. Wherever I felt there was too much exposition, I converted some into dialogue. Wherever a respondent jumped to conclusions, I provided a logical path to those conclusions. Where I saw abstracts, I made up inconsequential concrete details. A few respondents wrote in jargon, and I converted it to layman's terms.

I edited to make the stories accessible to the largest number of readers.

However, I did not change the heart nor the soul of any of the stories. I also did not add any of the folk sayings or folk saying references that are present in the stories, such as:

"happily ever after"

"Why buy the cow if you get the milk for free?"

"Why fix it if it ain't broke?"

"living in a fairy tale" and

"Marriage is just a piece of paper."

Because of the strict rules of the writing site where I collected them, I received and had to pay for 10 stories which did not ring true for me. I couldn't prove they weren't true, and they met the letter of the assignment, so I had to accept and pay for them. I didn't include them in this book. For all I know, I may have ended up including some stories that were fabricated. Only the respondents know for sure. I also received and paid for 3 stories which were too sad to include in this anthology.

I hope this book appeals to not-yet-married women and to their mothers, whom I hope gift this book to their single daughters.

I hope this book helps unmarried women turn their boyfriends into husbands.

A note on Conclusions

I'm almost 50 years old now, and I'm a trained teacher. I'm tempted to lecture you in this book. I'm tempted to read between the lines of all these true stories that I've collected from women who have managed to get their boyfriends to marry them, to cull out and spell out what they did that worked and what they did that was foolish. I'm tempted to beat you over the head with it.

In short: I'm tempted to tell you what to do.

I remember when I was young, though. No one could tell me what to do! Well, they could, but it was a waste of breath. I had a mind of my own, and I was determined to use it. I thought I was smarter than all the older people who were always trying to give me advice.

Fortunately, the 50th woman to give me her story threw in all the advice I would have given you, anyway! I hope you take it to heart. She's been married for twenty years, which is two years longer than I have, so she did something right when she got him to marry her.

I'm going to resist the temptation to tell you how to interpret these women's true stories. I'm just going to present them in the best possible light and let you read between the lines to figure out how to get him to marry you. These 50 true stories represent women from many walks of life, so you should find at least one you can identify with. Enjoy!

A Note on Conclusions

#1 SANDY AND JACK

I got tired of waiting for my boyfriend Jack to propose to me. We had been together for two years, and he hadn't even mentioned the 'm' word to me. If things had been left up to Jack, we would have been boyfriend and girlfriend for the rest of our lives. I had just turned thirty and could not wait much longer to be married. I knew I had to do something to push him along.

First, I tried giving him a taste of the good side of married life.

Jack was raised in a family where two people should not be together if they were not married. I could not just move myself in and wait for him to do the rest, as many of my girlfriends were doing with their boyfriends, in hopes of getting that 'm' word mentioned. I figured I had to slowly make myself a fixture in his apartment. When he got home from work and called, I would suggest going to his place instead of going out. I started to do some housework for him. I would tell him how messy his place was and offered to help him clean it up. I would wash the dishes and vacuum. After about two weeks of "giving him a taste of the good side of married life," nothing changed. I even did the unthinkable and cleaned his bathroom. All I got for that was a "Thanks, I owe you one." I had to come up with another idea that was more intensive.

I started leaving some of my things in his apartment.

I started small, with my slippers. I brought a pair

over and left them there so I could wear them when I came over. Next, I brought an extra set of clothing for work, just in case I was too tired to go back to my place and crashed on his couch overnight. I hung them in his closet. I put some candles around to get rid of the man smell and add a feminine touch. He seemed pretty good with all this, so I took the next step.

I brought a box of tampons over and left them under his bathroom sink for storage.

When he saw them, I got a strange look. I thought he was going to object, but he put them back and did not bring the subject up again. Finally, about a week after the tampon incident, Jack brought up the subject of marriage. He was joking around at first.

"With all your stuff around, people are going to start to think that you're my wife!"

This was it, the opening I needed to plant the seed of the idea I hoped would grow in his mind.

"Well, what about it? What do you think of me actually being your wife?"

"I love you, but I want to be sure we will last forever before we do anything about marriage. I don't believe in divorce, so when I marry it will be 'till death do us part'. I have to make very sure I am with the right person before I take a chance on that."

I felt relief. There was hope. His hesitation had nothing to do with me. It was his own doubt about himself and his ability to commit.

I told him, "I understand, and I'll give you some more time. I agree that I would not want to go through a separation and that if we marry, it will be 'till death do us part.'"

I left the items there that were already in his apartment, but I did not bring anything else over. We sat and talked, and I agreed to give him more time and a little more space. About six months passed without the mention of marriage.

Then one day I got the ultimate surprise. When I got home from work, there was takeout Chinese food waiting for me. Jack was there with a smile on his face. I opened the container, and instead of my favorite beef and broccoli there was a ring in a box. Jack even got down on one knee and proposed. We finally got married in the year 2005, in the springtime. We had a traditional wedding with all our family there.

Many people have asked us why we didn't live together. Well, Jack is a traditional man with some old-school values. He would not have wanted that, and his mother would have never spoken to him again. I did not want to live together because if we do eventually have children I want them to have the same last name and come from a married couple. I do not want people to look down on them or have to explain why their parents are not married. I also felt marriage means commitment. When getting married, you are agreeing to be with someone for the rest of your life. This shows that a person is dedicated and committed. I hope my story will help another woman build the courage to speak to her man about marriage.

#2 CRYSTAL AND PAUL

I hadn't been on campus three days before I met the man I was going to marry. I didn't know that he would be my future husband at the time. In fact, I never thought that he would even ask me out. Our last names, Palmer and Roop, placed us next to one another on the seating chart for English 101. I knew I would never be able to focus on subjects, verbs, and direct objects because the muscular, six-foot, sandy-haired Texan in the chair next to mine was the only subject I was interested in.

He was smart, too: a mechanical engineering major who got straight A's almost effortlessly. But what really attracted me to him was his sweet personality. You haven't lived until a boy a year older than you constantly refers to you as "Ma'am." The poor country boy was so nervous around women; he had no idea what a prize specimen he was.

Anyway, I never thought that this shy, sweet hunk would ever ask me out. But that certainly wasn't going to prevent me from flirting with him. What can I say? I was seventeen and single, and he was eighteen and hot. I always arrived early to our first-period English class just so we would have a few minutes to talk.

Unbeknownst to me, he thought I was a nice, sweet girl and wanted to ask me to go with him to a college event. But by midterms, he still hadn't mustered up the courage.

There was nothing I could do to make him ask me

out. I was old-fashioned, and if we were meant to be, I wanted the man to be the one to ask. Since I am married to the man, you know that he eventually did. Three weeks before the end of the semester, he practically knocked me off my chair by asking me to go with him to the Thanksgiving play that the school put on every year.

Our relationship moved pretty slow for the next few years. We were still young, and in college, so neither of us was in a big hurry.

At first.

By my senior year, I was so ready to get married. It seemed like everyone in our graduating class was engaged except for us, and we were the only couple that had been together since freshman year. I was dropping so many hints about marriage that I was sure I would get in trouble for littering. I mean, I'd had the wedding planned in my mind since sophomore year; if we waited any longer, the engagement would seem like an afterthought.

But Paul was not ready to commit.

"But we're still so young," he would argue, and "you're the first person I've ever dated."

"But that doesn't automatically mean that we aren't right for each other," I would argue back. "It's not like there's some rule that you have to date x number of people before you meet the right one, or that it's impossible to meet her before you reach a certain age. If we're right for each other, then we're actually really lucky because we've avoided painful breakups and years of loneliness."

While he couldn't argue with my logic, I did not receive a ring any time soon.

He saw no reason to rush into an engagement while we were both perfectly happy dating. To him, an engagement wasn't necessary to keep me exclusively his because the guys at our college would steer clear of a girl if they so much as saw her walking down the sidewalk with another guy.

As a girl, I was not so fortunate. At our small, private college, girls outnumbered the guys at least 4 to 1. In the minds of all the single gals on campus, the fact that Paul and I had been dating ever since freshman year was no deterrent. They would flirt with him every opportunity they had until we were engaged. I was eaten up with jealousy any time he mentioned the name of another girl.

What I did not know then was that jealousy is the glue that holds dating relationships together. Soon, I found out how powerful jealousy was.

Like I said, most guys typically ignored me because they knew I was Paul's girlfriend. But one day, I was sitting outside the school cafeteria waiting for Paul to join me for lunch when Kevin, a pre-med I knew from economics class, came up and put his arm around me! I was kinda creeped out by this. He'd never even talked to me before, and I knew he already had a girlfriend. Three, actually. So I had no idea what was wrong with him.

Kevin started stroking my hair, and saying, "You have pretty, pretty, brown hair. It looks like chocolate. You have pretty, pretty brown hair."

I found out later that Kevin had come down with a really bad cold and wanted to take some cough syrup but didn't have a teaspoon to measure the dosage with. So Kevin, the wonder-genius, concluded that his swallows were approximately a teaspoon each. Consequently, he had gulped an undefined amount of the stuff and was now drunker than beer-can chicken.

Possession of alcohol was against the rules at our

small college, so as Paul approached us, he never suspected that Kevin would be wasted, and he was livid. Paul yanked Kevin off me, shook him like a possessed maniac, and yelled:

"What do you think you're doing? Crystal and I are engaged!"

And that, girlfriends, was how Paul proposed.

Pinning him down to an exact date for our wedding was a little trickier. He kept flitting from let's-do-it-quick-and-get-it-over-with to let's-put-it-off-for-as-long-as-possible. But since he was from Texas and I was from Boston, I simply informed him that I was not going to leave my entire family and travel across a continent unless I had a marriage certificate, signed and dated.

We were married October 1, 2008 on a gorgeous autumn day in Boston, Massachusetts. As it turns out, I was right. By marrying young, the only thing we missed out on were unhappy years before finding each other. We are both so excited that we get to spend such a huge portion of our lives together.

#3 LIZZIE AND CORDELL

I'd been living with my boyfriend in Philadelphia for a couple of years. He's still studying architecture, but back then I was working at a dead-end office job, condemned to a life of servitude to support him through it. I was getting tired of this, but there didn't seem to be an end in sight, especially since he wanted to spend a semester in China, driving us further into debt. (Even though the Chinese yuan is six for our dollar, I still had to continue paying for our Philly apartment and car while we weren't using them.)

I'd like to say I put up with this solely because I'm in love with him, but I also didn't know what I wanted to do for a living. I'd planned to go to law school, but it costs about $150,000 for 3 years, and then I would continue with the life of servitude. For a lack of better plans, and out of concern about Cordell meeting even more Asian babes over there than he seemed to be meeting in architecture school in Philly, I went to China with him.

Many of the girls there are really traditional. When I was teleworking from the coffee shop (it served a lot of milk tea), I struck up a lot of conversations with them. I showed them Cordell's picture, and they oohed, and they ahhed. They asked me if I was going to marry him.

So I went back to our (crappy) apartment and exploded.

"Why won't you marry me?"

"Because," Cordell answered, "I don't have any

money."

"You can't be serious. *That*'s the reason?"

"I already have a kid, Lizzie. I want to do the wedding right this time. I have no money, and I owe back child-support payments out the wazoo. I can't get married like this. I'm a scrub."

"I wouldn't be here with you if you were a scrub. If you were a scrub, I would be back in Nebraska with my old boyfriend!"

This last part was a little bit of a fib. My old boyfriend dressed as a ninja, could not hold down a job, and had "Jedi" as his religious affiliation on Facebook. But Cordell wouldn't marry me.

The feminists told me to leave. My friends told me to leave. My parents told me I was going to go even more into debt than I already was with my college loans. But I didn't leave. I'd gone all this way with him, and I was going to see it through.

The solution to my problem came from where I least expected it.

When I worked in the office back in Philly, my plebeian office job took about 8.5 hours a day. When I did my work online, it took four hours a day, at the most. Now, I've never been the type to know what to do with my free time, but I had so much of it now that I joined an anime fan group at a bar in Beijing. (I never go to bars, either.)

I befriended guys there who had similar interests. Now, keep in mind:

1) My American office salary of 42k equaled about 252k in China.

2) I'm not bad looking.

3) I was an intriguing ethnic anomaly there.

4) My employers said my productivity had increased, so they weren't nagging me to come back to the office.

With those four points there, you have another recipe for my leaving Cordell. But again, I did not.

Many anime types, there as well as here, have unconventional interests. One of the girls made Chinese wedding dresses. They're nothing like the white mainstay frocks you see in the States. Chinese wedding dresses are short, sexy, and inspired by cartoons. All are white or in pastel colors. Plus, they're silk. It's cheaper to get silk there, so Mao-ling had a ton of silk garments.

"How come your stuff is so cute here?" I asked Mao-ling.

She looked at me like I was crazy.

I said, "Cute isn't big where I live. I think it's the strong, independent woman thing."

"It's always been," she said, "and people buy it. People buy it where you are, too."

"Really." I challenged.

Mao-ling is an artist and doesn't have much of a head for business. I'm very organized, but I'm really not all that creative. She and I split her design business 50/50. I set up store accounts on eBay and Etsy, and I got a few brick and mortar stores in Philadelphia to carry her dresses through a friend of mine in PhillyU's fashion program. After about six months, they were selling beautifully. I think the reason these clothes sell so well in the States is the same reason men like Asian girls: they're "cuter" and a bit more delicate, in appearance at least.

If you count the money I get from private clients,

Chinese stores, and the accessories I sell online, I make about 20k more per year in business for myself than I did with my regular job. I also saved about 15k from that my first few weeks.

I am so much happier as a business owner than I was as a corporate desk jockey that I became a whole lot easier to get along with, and Cordell magically found a whole lot more time for me in his schedule.

Now that I was more successful, I told Cordell I was going to leave if he didn't marry me, but first, on a hunch, I used the 15k I had saved to pay off Cordell's back child support.

And Cordell, like me, was able to think a whole lot more clearly now that most of the pressures in his life were gone.

I may not be a strong, independent woman based on this story, but I got married in 2011, and we're going on 2 years now. He has a half-scholarship, and I pay the rest of his tuition as well as our bills by running my business full time and consulting with my office part-time. We'll be a power couple by next summer.

#4 BROOK AND MATI

I got married in January of 2006 to my soul mate, Mati. I was a 20 year old virgin at the time, and I remained faithful to my vow to remain pure until marriage. My husband was reluctant to get married because he feared being monogamous to one woman forever.

We began dating in 2004, in a long distance relationship as we were attending colleges in different states. I finished my degree program in two years, and he was just about done with his four year program.

My dream was to be a stay-at-home mom and have at least six kids. He knew that from day one, and now I thought it was time for us to get married because he had already been working full time for three years, and we both had money saved.

His two objections were that he felt that he was too young to get married and some of his friends had kids but were not married. He was 25 at the time. His friends had a huge influence on him because they had grown up together. This created friction between me and his friends. My parents did not like that he waffled with his feelings about me. He asked me to live with him, but I refused to without a commitment.

One day, his mother Viola became very ill. She suffered a bad kidney infection, and he could not see her because she lived in Kenya. I knew he was struggling, and sadly he began to act out and party hard in the scene with his friends. I knew his emotions were out of whack because of the situation with his mother.

His behavior made me really emotional. We had a big discussion.

I told him, "I still want you for a husband, but I don't want you to regret marrying me."

His face wrinkled up like he might cry. "Why would I ever regret marrying you?"

I told him my family's secrets:

"I am someone whose parents were married in the 80's because my mother's parents forced her to marry her baby's father. I always felt like a burden to my father. He was forced into marriage at 19 by his very religious parents and had to work a job at a local store instead of attending college to become a veterinarian like he wanted. I don't want my future children to feel as though their father was backed against the wall just to score a lifelong marriage commitment and a one carat diamond engagement ring."

That made an impression on him, but another big event happened before he proposed.

He was out at a club at 4 am with some friends when he got hit in the head with a beer bottle and suffered other injuries. He was badly injured and had to stay in the hospital for a few days. I was irate at him for having gotten into that situation. Apparently, a friend of his was called a racial slur, so he stepped in to defend him and ended up getting assaulted.

He called me, and I refused to go to the hospital.

I said, "Fighting is something that I cannot condone. It makes me see you as someone who is immature." I hung up, and I did not return his calls or texts for 10 days.

After he got out of the hospital, he managed to enter my upstairs apartment's bedroom window by climbing a ladder. I was not home at the time, but my neighbors were. They called and alerted me to the fact that a man wearing a sling and a bandage on his head was climbing through my window. I told them not to call the cops and that it was my former boyfriend, Mati.

I was angry and ready for a confrontation with him. However, when I arrived home, I saw my apartment covered in candles and rose petals. He had a CD playing with my favorite music and on the TV he had stuck a poster that said:

"Will you marry me?"

I said, "No way! You think you can settle for me now, but I know you won't be monogamous. Your friends are always going to be influencing you to get in more fights. We're just going to eventually drift apart. That is not the life I want."

He told me, "I really want to make this work. You are who I want. I'm not settling for you. When I was in the ambulance, going to the ER, the one thing I wished was that you were there with me, holding my hand."

We kissed a lot, and then I told him, "I'll only marry you if you agree to be 100% honest and refrain from fighting."

He told me that the only thing that he would ever fight for is my heart.

I then agreed to marry him, and I put on the custom designed engagement ring that he bought me.

#5 JESSICA AND STU

I was the last one of my group of girlfriends to get married. I was thirty-two and childless. I had been in a long term relationship for seven years, and it was so volatile that I knew there was no way I was going to marry him. Leaving that relationship was something I should have done for a while, but it was very hard for me to leave my first real relationship. Anyway, I met my husband one day after work when I got off the train to go home. He was one of those taxi drivers that hung out there, looking for customers.

At first, I thought, "Oh no, I hope he is not trying to be anything other than friends!"

Because, I was not into guys who were not professional or working towards a career. I honestly could not see myself going to my sorority soirees and bringing him along. He somehow always seemed to be at the train station whenever I got off the train, and soon we started talking. He was funny, and I had not expected that. I had noticed that he was kind of cute, too. Well, not just kind of cute; he was handsome.

I did not expect to say yes when he asked me if I wanted to go and get something to eat, but I did say yes. I liked talking to him. Maybe because his experiences were so different from the guys I usually dated. They had all gone to college, pledged a fraternity, graduated, gone into their chosen field, and tried to make the best of it. I wasn't used to someone who hadn't finished high school and had been working for himself as a cab driver for as long as he had.

We continued to see each other for about nine months, and then I found out I was pregnant. His first reaction was not what I expected.

"I'm not ready for a child."

"I don't understand. Why not?"

"It's too much responsibility. I'm too young for that."

"You're only two years younger than I. You have a job and an apartment, so you know how to be responsible." I was devastated. The child was on his way, ready or not.

Nonetheless, I was thrilled to finally be pregnant. I already loved my baby.

The day our son was born, his father was nowhere to be found. When he finally showed up at the hospital, I was livid. His excuse was not good enough, and I let him know it. When I saw him with his son though, my heart softened. We decided to move in together and try to make it work.

We lived together for a year, and I thought we would eventually get around to talking of marriage. However, whenever I would bring it up, he would say the most ridiculous statements. He said things such as:

"I'm not ready for that," and

"I want to be in a better financial position before I take on a marriage."

My thought was, "He wants to have the best of both worlds."

He always hung out with his friends on the weekends, and that was the cause of a lot of arguments between us. I felt our situation was already one of a family unit, so becoming husband and wife was the next logical step. As far as being financially secure, we both worked and split the bills in half. I knew he was afraid of committing fully when he did not even want to have a bank account together.

Our fighting got so bad that we ended up leaving each other.

Two years later, our son was three and getting into trouble at school. I felt that he was too young to be getting in trouble and that it was because his father needed to be more present in his life. We sat down and had a talk about it.

He told me, "I want to be there for my son, and I do miss being with you. There's a missing aspect in my life, and I want to give us another try."

I told him, "The only way I'll let you back into my heart and my home is as my husband."

We started out slowly this time around. We had been dating again for about ten months when he asked me to marry him. I asked God to help me make the right decision and accepted his proposal. We got married in 2004.

While our road has not always been smooth, we are doing OK. We now have two children and feel that we have what it takes to make our marriage last.

#6 MARIE AND FRED

Fred and I met online. It was 2010, and it had taken me 3 years to finally get to the place where I felt it was time to move on after being rejected by the father of my child. I had all the usual uncertainties about meeting someone online, but I was a stay-at-home mom and nanny, and I didn't have the opportunity to get out much. So, I put my doubts on the back burner and took the plunge.

After a week of getting private messages from obvious dirt bags and scoundrels, I got a different kind of message. He wanted to strike up a conversation, not just get my number. I could tell he had actually read my profile and taken the time to appreciate the honesty that I had tried to put into telling someone about myself.

Fred and I started private messaging back and forth. At first, our messages were short, only a paragraph or two, but as we continued to write they grew, pages and pages, sometimes two messages a day. There was this one message when we knew we were perfect for each other.

I wrote, "I have a friend who is now a DR."

In his reply, he wrote the most random thing ever: "You mean a D.R. Trimmer Mower?"

I about died laughing. He got me! He had my same sense of humor: random and silly. A few months later, we were talking about that message. He said he debated whether or not he should write that.

He told me, "First, I thought, 'No, she might not get it, and I'll look like and idiot,' but then I thought, 'If she does get it, then she is perfect for me.'"

Funny how something that at the time seemed so silly and just so tiny can mean that much. Well, after private messaging for six months, finally we exchanged phone numbers, and that of course led to us meeting.

Fred lived 2 hours away, so we met in the middle. I remember the first time I met him. I knew what he looked like of course, from pictures, but pictures never do anyone but the perfect any justice. He's tall, dark and handsome with blue eyes, my favorite! It was the best first date I ever had. We were like the best of old friends meeting for the first time. It was magical. Fred and I continued to talk over the phone every day, and to this day have still not gone a single day without speaking to each other.

Having been divorced a couple years earlier, Fred was very cautious when it came to love. He knew the devastating effects that taking love and relationships lightly can have on a person, and how taking love as a flighty emotion could affect us as a couple.

But I wore him down.

As our conversations and visits continued over the months, we grew in trust. I never gave him a reason to doubt his trust in me, and neither did he give me reason to doubt him. That trust helped him overcome the doubts that were there from the failure of his first marriage. Truth, honesty, and we have never wavered in our honesty in who we are to each other. I can truthfully say that Fred has always been Fred. I can always depend on him to tell me the truth, and he can always expect me to get upset if it is not something I want to hear, but he knows I will calm down and become logical, because that is who I am.

We never missed a day speaking to each other,

and we never canceled our visits. I knew how important it was to him for me to keep a promise, even in the little things, such as making a phone call when a call was promised.

After 6 months of dating, we both just knew. There was no way that we would ever find someone who was more perfect for each of us than we were for each other. Unfortunately, we still lived 2 hours away from each other, and we had agreed to save ourselves for marriage, but we missed each other daily, and it was getting harder and harder to have to wait two weeks to see each other. The visits were getting harder to end, and I found myself just not wanting to come home when I went to visit, and he would procrastinate leaving when he came to visit me. We knew something had to change.

He'd say things like, "Why don't you move closer?"

I'd explain, "It's highly impractical for me to uproot my life and change jobs just to look for another apartment on my own." I insisted, "That would cause severe un-needed stress on me and my son," especially since Fred and I knew we were just made for each other.

I held my ground. I was not going to move or change my life for any man who was not my husband.

Fred planned the date for weeks. It could not have been any more perfect, like he is for me. I will always remember it. It was Valentine's Day, and we were meeting for dinner. He took me to the same lovely restaurant where we met the first time. Then we went to the park where we'd gone on our first date. It was a beautiful snowy night, and he got down on one knee in the middle of the playground and asked me to be his for the rest of our lives, to make each other laugh every day and to never have to leave each other's side again.

After talking about it and telling each other that we wanted to stay pure, we decided that a long engagement was not needed. We had never had even a second of doubt that we were who we said we were, and that we would be compatible. Not that there wouldn't be an adjustment period after we got married. It takes some adjustment and compromise to get used to living with another person. So, we were married in July, 2012, just a year after I got that first message from that man who was not like the rest.

#7 MICHEAL AND SHYAN DOOBERMAN

Have you heard the story about the man who promised to buy a milk cow? The man told the owner he would buy the cow, but he wanted a sample first, to make sure the milk was good. After he got the sample, the man said, "Ah! That's good, thank you! I'll be back tomorrow." This went on and on, day after day. The man showed up every day for free milk, but never would buy the cow.

After four beautiful years of being with the man that I loved so much, I finally persuaded him to marry me. I didn't find out until recently why he was dodging the old "ball 'n' chain," but once I found out, a part of me somewhat understood why he was afraid to marry me. He was scared we would end up like his parents: divorced and miserable. He has recently expressed this personal fear to me time and time again. Plus, it didn't help that his last girlfriend left him standing at the altar, which crushed his entire being. It took me a long time to gain his trust, and that is one of the reasons why I was so willing to wait four long years for an engagement ring.

At first, I thought it was me. I thought he had no desire to be with me for the rest of his life. Of course, there were past events that I felt could have contributed to his fear of marriage, but I thought we were over those days.

I figured If I was willing to sit through the midnight nose picking and the loud burps at the dinner table, then why not take on those bodily mishaps forever? Honestly, I thought they were cute, so cute that I would laugh every time he did something so disgusting. Contrary to popular belief, these are the things that make a marriage work. Accepting a person for who they are and what they bring to the table has been part of my Christian upbringing all of my life. I believe that's why it was so easy for me to confront him about getting married. I finally became so comfortable in my faith as well as my beliefs that I was no longer accepting the lifestyle of fornication.

Me being the type of woman that I am, I don't believe that you should give the milk away for free. Plus, he knew for well over two years that I wanted to marry him.

I finally decided to confront him without actually confronting him. Date night is special in our relationship, so I made sure that I picked the perfect movie. I went into my arsenal and chose a chick flick that would be a tear jerker for me, and a reality check for him. *The Five-Year Engagement* was perfect because it gave me a platform to stand on and express how I felt about our relationship, where it was headed, and how we could change it.

Of course, he had complaints about the chosen movie. I had expected that. But, he sat through it with me. Once the movie was over, I explained my position.

"Marriage is what I want, and if it's not going to happen, then we're headed in two different directions."

He laughed at the idea of me trying to be confrontational.

I guessed he didn't believe I was serious about not settling for a situation that didn't make me happy.

But, that night I felt in my heart that I was serious, and I was. I moved back with my old roommate that next weekend. Michael and I stayed apart for well over 3 months. During those three months, I decided to date and move on.

He was hell bent against getting married, and said he was more than willing to accept the separation.

Fortunately for me, I knew he would eventually agree to get married, which is why the short break was easy for me to handle. I knew he wouldn't be able to live without me for too long. I was the only real thing he had in this world. We completed each other, but that was something that I needed for him to realize.

Of course, there was a small part of me that was afraid he wasn't going to take me back, but I chased that fear away with the company of other people.

A little after the 3 month break up, I was to the point where I had given up on whatever relationship we did have. I hadn't talked to Micheal. He hadn't called me, so I figured that "we" no longer existed. It was a Saturday night, and I had been in the house all week. I'd spent my vacation eating Hot Pocket pizzas and waffles with ice cream on top, which was something I used to do with Micheal. I'd cried so much during that past week and used so many tissues that I scoured online to see if I could possibly invest in Kleenex. My chick flicks had become re-runs, and I had no passion to spend time with anyone, except for Micheal.

Feeling sorry for myself for well over 3 hours, I finally hopped into my bed. A few minutes afterward, I heard ticking sounds on my window, which for a while I mistook for rain. Mind you, my Micheal had never been the romantic type. I'd always seen him as the dorky, shy type who loved to keep things simple.

Well, that night he broke my window trying to be romantic, and it actually worked.

On any other day, I would have been highly upset. On that night, I was mopping my heart up off the floor. I felt like Juliet, and he was my Romeo.

Down on one knee, he fluently spoke original poetry. Surrounding him was a pile of pink and red rose petals, along with the cutest puppy I had ever seen.

I was pretty puzzled about the puppy, but when he sent the puppy to my door, I noticed a ring on the collar.

As soon as Micheal realized I'd seen the ring, he asked me to marry him.

This encounter led to one of the most beautiful winter weddings in the history of weddings, and we were married on Dec 8th, 2012. I can honestly say that I knew he would come back to me, eventually. I knew that we were made for each other. I knew that this world wouldn't be able to keep us apart. When God pairs two souls, nothing can come between them.

OK, maybe I had a small amount of doubt that night I ate entire boxes of waffles and Hot Pockets, but for the most part, my womanly intuition told me that he knew better than to let this good thing get away.

#8 LAYLA AND JAMIE

When I first met Jamie, I knew there was a chance he was the future husband that I had been looking everywhere for. There was a long list of characteristics I wanted in my future husband—and yes, I'd written them all down:

1. Musical

2. Outgoing and interesting

3. Loves God

4. Shares my sense of humor

5. Is a leader to me

6. Knows how to handle my strong personality

7. Keeps me grounded

8. Has dark hair and dark eyes

What was funny was that I met so few men who met every single one of these qualifications. I knew when I met the man I was destined to marry, he'd stick out like a sore thumb.

The first night we hung out, I immediately realized that he was hilarious and naturally a funny person; he loved talking to people and initiated conversation with me. Of course, he also had rich dark hair and eyes. It killed me when he brought out a guitar and started playing Eric Clapton's "Layla." All the white flags were waving.

After becoming close friends over the next six months, Jamie and I had a connection and knew there was something special between us. He told me he felt like he had known me his whole life and that he could let all his walls down around me. I didn't tell him, but I felt exactly the same way. After finally admitting our feelings to each other, we kept the relationship a secret, which was plenty of fun, and then made it public with our community and friends a few weeks later.

Although I'd like to say I was the patient type, I'd be lying if I pretended I was patient for him to propose. After a mere month of dating, marriage was all we talked about at times, and we likely rushed everything too much.

There were a few things holding us back from getting married—mainly one: money. Jamie was working part-time and couldn't seem to hold down a steady job. The lack of motivation on his part made me frustrated, and I began to believe the lie that marriage would never come for us. My biological clock was ticking, and I wanted at least a few years of marriage before kids came along.

We lived 45 minutes away from each other in Southern California, which made it difficult when we didn't have time to go see each other. I declined whenever he wanted me to spend the night or stay for a few days at his house because I knew that would only make our relationship worse and cause problems. I wanted to wait until we were married to live together, and I wasn't going to compromise that goal just because I was impatient for a wedding ring.

Jamie seemed to be perfectly content procrastinating on popping the question. He seemed to enjoy lazy days watching football or going to hang out with the guys more than the work required to progress towards marriage.

I would get frustrated at times and finally told him, "You need to gain a better work ethic, if you want to keep me in your life!"

He insisted, "I'll find a stable, full-time job eventually."

The word 'eventually' stung. Why wasn't he as anxious to marry me as I was to marry him? Because he didn't have a biological clock, that's why. That word, 'eventually,' made his whole statement seem meaningless and empty.

Maybe I should've stuck to my guns and left him. Maybe we would've gotten married sooner. Maybe.

The thing was: except for the lack of work ethic and his propensity for procrastination, everything about Jamie was perfect; our relationship was incredibly romantic and beautiful, and he was my best friend. But our dreams of marriage were on hold until he chose to move into maturity.

I think everything came into place for us when I learned to be content with my circumstances and stop thinking about marriage every day. I prayed that God would give me patience and allow me to enjoy being single until it was time for Jamie and I to get engaged. I needed to stop looking at all my friends who were headed down the aisle and needed to break the habit of comparing myself. I wasn't missing out on anything, and I wasn't about to force someone to marry me if they weren't ready. Prayer is what finally worked on Jamie gaining full-time employment and maturing. I think he needed to do it for himself before anyone else.

After he got his real job, Jamie told me, "I'm sorry for all the fights we had about my career goals. I have a tendency to be lazy due to the examples of older people in my life."

The day Jamie proposed was one that I wasn't

expecting. He brought me up to the top of a hill in Orange County to overlook the city.

I lost my earring on the way up.

He said, "This will make for a funny story to tell our kids later in life!"

And then Jamie gave me a letter he wrote that was strung with plenty of humor and incredible words telling me how much I meant to him and how I had changed his life.

My mascara was running halfway down my face by the time I found the ring he bought for me, hiding within one of the gifts he gave me with the letter. It had my mother's original wedding diamond in the ring.

He was like a little kid who couldn't wait to see my reaction to it.

A few days after our engagement, I was laid off from my job and panicking as I looked for stable work. Jamie was behind me every step of the way with job applications and encouraging me that the right opportunity would come along. He didn't belittle me for failing to keep my job, the way some would. He was fully supportive and had faith that our future was intact.

I was able to gain full-time employment where Jamie also works. He has his hard days where he doesn't feel motivated, but all-in-all he's incredibly hardworking and has a high amount of ethics and appreciation for his position. It's teaching me to work diligently, even when there's no one around.

Today, we have been married close to a year, and it's been an incredible beginning to our marriage. I know our marriage wouldn't have been as successful or intact if we had lived together, and we wouldn't have honored each other in doing so. The way he stays positive about his current job and sets goals for himself has taught me to do the same for myself and to be truly proud of my work ethic. I'm now eager and excited to watch Jamie accomplish all of his dreams and teach me along the way.

#9 TRISHA AND DAVID

I married the love of my life, David, in 1991. Marriage was not popular at this time in our society, and it was even more unappealing in our private circle. People were into living together and having babies without the thought of getting married; many of our peers had been together for years and had multiple children without the benefit of holy matrimony.

David and I met through an unusual place: the local church bingo hall. That's right...the bingo hall! I've loved the game of bingo since I was a child, and our church sponsored bingo games twice a week.

Looking back, I think I was this close to having a gambling problem. I justified my bingo fever because the proceeds went to the charitable endeavors of our parish. When I lost, I comforted myself with the knowledge that our church was funding a domestic violence shelter and providing substance abuse rehabilitation. This was all-important because the crack epidemic was ravishing our community of the Bronx, New York at the time. When I won, I contributed a tenth of my winnings back to the church and went shopping.

Before I met David, I met his mother. This association, very simply, was the key to getting David to marry me: I befriended his mother! Although three years passed from the time we met until we married, my relationship with David's mother sealed the deal!

I met Dorothy at the bingo hall, although I was familiar with her from church. Dorothy had a heart-felt dream to move back to her home town of Franklin, VA, into a house built from the ground up. In order to put her children through school, Dorothy held a variety of low-paying jobs after her husband died in the late seventies. To accomplish her dream, Dorothy sold food at the bingo games. That is how we bonded.

I left work in a hurry on Tuesdays and Thursdays to get to bingo. I was always hungry when I got there, and Dot's Spot in the bingo hall was *the* place to get good food. The menu varied each day and was a mixture of pre-cooked dishes and cook-to-order items. Fried chicken, fish, and burgers were cooked to perfection as they were ordered. Macaroni and cheese, vegetables of all varieties, and entrees like spaghetti, meatloaf, pot roast, and barbeque ribs were cooked in advance and served to the bingo players. In addition to these mouth-watering offerings, Dot was an extraordinary baker. She had cupcakes, brownies, sweet potato and apple pies, and all kinds of cakes for sale by the slice. You could also place a private order, and she would bake a specialty just for you.

I met Dot personally by ordering a strawberry cheesecake for the baby shower of a (single) friend. Dot was a friendly woman with a winning personality; while I was placing my order, she was telling me of her aspirations. It appeared that Dot's business had been growing, and she was becoming tired as well as having health concerns. She had five children whom she wanted to pass the business on to, but none of them were interested. She needed help, as the volume of her business was expanding, but she was a trooper. The bottom fell out when the bingo hall added another day to the festivities. When the parish added Saturday nights to the schedule, Dot made me an offer. She asked me to be her assistant at

Dot's Spot—a slot she couldn't get any of her five children to accept.

I began by going to her apartment and helping her prepare dishes and bake her wonderful cakes and pies. There, I met her children. They didn't know what to make of me. On the one hand, they were grateful that somebody was helping their mother, since they didn't want to. On the other hand, they appeared suspicious of my motives and jealous of the amount of time I spent with Dot.

I flourished during this time. I had lost my own mother when I was twelve; now I finally had someone to have the 'big girl' conversations with. We talked about God, men, life, friends, and a variety of other topics. Dorothy and I helped each other tremendously. She picked my brain in order to understand her children; I used her mother wit and caring to nourish myself in a way I had never experienced.

Sadly, Dot's children were all into drugs. I saw this immediately but broke it to her gently. I don't think she really believed me until her beloved twin boys David and Darien were arrested and convicted of possession with intent to sell. She dipped into her home savings and got a good lawyer for her then twenty-five year old sons. They got eighteen months.

Dot seemed to do prison time right along with her sons, and the time did not agree with her. I became her closest confidante: she revealed to me that she had serious heart disease and would have to have double bypass surgery. She would not tell her children, but she told me. Her fondest desire was to be living in her home in Franklin by then. She had already broken ground and begun the construction. By then, I was almost running Dot's Spot in the bingo hall. I no longer had time to play my favorite game; I was too busy serving the customers.

When David came home from prison, he seemed to sense something wasn't right with his mom. Unlike his twin brother Darien, who returned to the street life, David stayed at his mom's home to take care of her. Her illness really changed him.

When I met David, it was love at first sight for me. He was originally amused by me: a church girl who was skin-tight with his mother. He was a bad boy, and I was not on his level at all. I watched from the side as he went through girlfriend after girlfriend. My relationship with his mother touched him, however, and he began to get to know me. We fell in love.

In January of 1990, Dot finished building her dream home and moved in. We left the Bronx and moved in with her (separate bedrooms of course). One year later, we got married! Dot was thrilled. In June of 1993, Dot had her bypass surgery. She did not survive. She left the house to David, and twenty years later we still live there. I moved from the horrors of the inner city to a sleepy town in Virginia and married the man of my dreams... all because I befriended his mother first.

#10 JULIE AND SAMUEL

When Samuel and I got married on July 9, 2011, we had only been together a little over a year, but I knew from the moment I met him that he was The One. We're both old fashioned, though, so I had to get him to realize we needed to get married and make him think the whole thing was his idea. It really took some doing, to be honest.

We were happy together, just dating, from April 2010 until the end of the year. Both of us were feeling pressure to spend the night together, but we held off until our wedding night (which made it that much nicer). Aside from sex, the idea of marriage just did not appeal to Samuel. He had a really bad childhood, with his real father treating his mother horribly and his step-father, later, becoming an alcoholic who was severely abusive to them all. In his mind, marriage was about pain and suffering, rather than happiness together.

I knew the truth, though: love could heal those wounds, and marriage between two people who truly love one another is wonderful. We loved each other deeply, and all that remained was convincing him that we needed to get married while still letting him (the manly man) think it was all his idea!

The whole process started in September of 2010, when I realized that if I wanted to spend the rest of my life with Samuel, I was going to have to make it happen. It was slow going, to be honest. I had to convince him, first, that marriage was the answer. That took a lot of me talking

49

about how my mom and dad had been together for more than 30 years, happily, in spite of their problems. More than once, I mentioned my grandparents, who were married for well over 50 years and had nine children together. A few times, I asked questions about some of his happily married relatives. There were quite a few casual conversations about what made all of these people so happy together, and over time he realized that love did not have to be about pain, hurt, and abuse, and that people could love one another for a lifetime.

As those wounds in his heart started to heal, I started talking about our own eventual marriage. At first, it was a casual mention here and there:

"If we were married, then you wouldn't have to take me home now."

Once, I asked him if he thought he might get married eventually.

He said, "Probably, if you ever want to."

I was thrilled! It wasn't a proposal, but it was a step in the right direction. So, I kept mentioning marriage off and on, making sure not to cause a scene or make a big deal out of it. I mean, I wasn't asking him to be my husband; I wanted him to propose marriage to me.

The conversations continued, and I was patient until New Year's Eve for 2011. We were out together celebrating the new year with friends at a big gathering. Well, Samuel had a couple glasses of wine too many before the countdown started, and as everyone started gathering for the big moment, he said it:

"We're getting married this year. How about July 4?"

I was floored! It wasn't the proposal I had been dreaming about since I was a little girl, but then again, it fit our relationship perfectly.

All I could do was smile, blush, and say, "OK!"

He started telling people around us that we had decided to get married, and we were congratulated by everyone.

As would become clear the next day, we went our separate ways that night with different things on our minds. Waking and remembering what had been said just before midnight, I decided to celebrate the new year by taking Samuel breakfast in bed. I went to his apartment with bagels and all the necessary ingredients for a lovely breakfast. He was awake when I got there, which ruined the surprise. However, what he said then almost ruined the relationship.

As we dined on bagels and orange juice, Samuel spoke about the night before, mentioning he was sorry for drinking so much wine. I told him it was fine, then asked if we needed to tell the rest of our families about our plans to get married.

"What plans?" he asked.

I reminded him about his "proposal" the night before.

He said he didn't remember that, and wasn't ready to get married.

I was crushed. I rushed out of his apartment, not knowing if I even wanted to continue the relationship. After going home and crying a while, I decided it was not the time to talk about it. We actually didn't talk for a couple of days, until he finally called and asked if I wanted to go to dinner.

I said, "OK," thinking we would have a chance to talk and decide if we even wanted to stay together.

For dinner that evening, we went back to the restaurant where we had our first date. We had been there several times since then, so I thought nothing of it, at least not until he pulled out the ring over a shared piece of chocolate swirled cheesecake at dessert.

"Julie, I want us to spend our lives together. Will you marry me?"

I was beyond shocked, but I said, "Yes!"

Turns out, the time without talking made him realize how much he missed me, and what he had done wrong. We were married later that same year, actually on July 9, just because the church was booked on the fourth. But the imperfect date went along with the imperfect proposal to make a perfect story for us to tell in the future. Oh, and I still let him think the whole thing was his idea, even though you and I know the truth.

#11 AMANDA AND MATTHEW

We had been dating for a year and half, and it had been tough! Our entire dating experience was during college, and we went to a small Christian college with strict rules. Any time we wanted to have a serious conversation or anything, it felt like someone was watching us just to get some juicy gossip to spread about our time alone together. Seriously! Clearly, any time a couple spends alone together, they must be doing something inappropriate. We, like all other couples on campus, were never allowed to be behind a closed door or out too late at night. The lights always had to be on. Our feet always had to be touching the floor. A lot of the time we would just sit on the floor to ensure that no foul play was suspected, so dating was sort of like being in a fishbowl with a mass of people watching. The pressures were ridiculous, but that drew us even closer, and eventually we started to talk about getting married.

Many of my friends thought living together was a more viable option. They would tell me:

"Living together is less committal."

"It's less expensive and can easily segue into getting married when you have enough money or confidence that the relationship should be permanent."

Some of my friends argued, "Getting married without having lived together is a dumb idea anyway because you don't really know someone very well until you've woken up next to them and their stinky morning breath."

But, my now-husband and I don't believe in sex before marriage. We also think that marriage and living together are complimentary changes that work best when done at the same time.

My now husband had some reservations about getting married. I remember very well a few conversations about whether or not it was the right time, since:

1) We were poor.

2) I had another semester of college left.

3) Dating had been so difficult.

4) He was especially concerned about us starting a family too soon if we got married right away.

After a lot of talking, I convinced him that I didn't want—and wasn't ready for—little ones for several years. That seemed to reassure him that getting married didn't mean having babies immediately! I also had to spend a lot of time telling him about my willingness to be poor for a while, and that really all I wanted was to be married to him for the rest of our lives! Part of our conversations about marriage had to do with openness, too. We had to be open to getting married when the time was right, not just doing it as soon as possible.

Luckily, it didn't take too much convincing for us not to live together before marriage. We had a lot of people in our lives who were really opposed to that lifestyle and who would have been disappointed in us had we done it. Plus, it just seemed dangerous emotionally to both of us! Living together is huge and takes a relationship to a very deep, personal, and vulnerable level. Neither of us wanted to be in that sort of a relationship without first having committed to each other for life through marriage.

So, long story short, in the summer of 2012, we got married! The ceremony was beautiful, and we were so overjoyed by the blessings of people who supported us in so many ways. Several people told us they were glad that we never lived together before we got married, and honestly, we were, too! We got married at the right time for us, and now we get to experience the joys, challenges, and adventure of living together within the secure boundaries of marriage.

#12 LISA AND JASON

My husband's cousin also recently asked me how I managed to get my husband to marry me. I have to admit, at first I was a little insulted. Is it not immediately obvious that I'm quite a catch, myself? After I swallowed my pride, we engaged in a discussion that made me look at myself and think about how it all happened.

The reason she was asking was that she was approaching a birthday and edging closer to 40 and was still not married and had no prospects in sight. She remembered my husband who, in his youth, had been very outspoken about his opinion that marriage was outdated and a silly convention. He had made his entire family aware that he never intended to get married. He believed that if two people love each other then they do not need a piece of paper to keep them together. Yes, he was quite the deep philosopher. After 15 years of marriage and 2 kids, I had kind of forgotten about his anti-marriage stance. I started wondering, "How *did* I manage to change his mind?"

When I look back now, I, too, wonder how we got together. We were very different people who had very different opinions about the world.

I was from an unconventional family. My childhood was not exemplary at all. My parents were young hippie types who really had no plan for creating a stable life for me and my brothers and sisters. Chaos was our lifestyle. We lived on a farm that I think they had planned on renovating and working, but never got around to it. We ended up living in a gutted out old farmhouse that had no interior finished walls, no indoor plumbing, no heat, and no plans for improvement.

One thing my mother managed to do right was to enroll my siblings and me in a decent private school that was free for members of her church. There, I saw the difference between my life and the lives of children from stable homes. I learned how valuable a stable marriage is for creating a life worth living. While my siblings and I never knew what to expect when we got home from school each night, our classmates were going to piano lessons, softball practice, and play dates. All my hopeful aspirations for childhood fun were kept to myself and quietly let go because we had no money, no stability, and no parental guidance.

I learned to be very skeptical about the promises of free love floating around in the 70's and decided that I would never take a chance on having children outside of marriage.

Strangely, my husband, the anti-marriage philosopher, was from a stable and loving family. His parents are still married today and seem to truly love each other. His childhood was full of parental involvement, family vacations, music lessons, sleepovers with numerous cousins, Sunday dinners with the grandparents... all the things I had missed out on as a child.

My husband never was against family. He had just somehow come to believe that marriage was not necessary in order to be a family. His philosophical mind had formed the conviction that two people should stay together because they love each other, not because they signed a paper in front of a judge.

When we met, we were teaching at the same

elementary school. Jason was an art teacher, and I was a special education teacher. I got to know him because he was assigned to cover my classroom when I went to lunch and whenever I had to meet with my students' parents. He would leave a record of the events that transpired in my absence, but they were never serious. They were hilarious!

"John gave a great impression of Mrs. Steagal: 'I'm warning you kids!'"

"Jessica and Sarah decided they needed to check everyone's stories about the hamster, since they both have hamsters and no one else does. You should have seen them walking around the room, hovering over everyone's papers. :)"

I started to look forward to those notes every day. I would share the funniest ones with my teaching assistants, and we would laugh out loud together.

One day, one of them asked me, "Do you think he's in love with you?"

I was shocked by that comment. It had never occurred to me.

Turns out, my teaching assistant was quite insightful. Jason and I had worked together for about 3 years and had kidded around and talked as friends and colleagues. I had noticed how cute he was, tall and blue eyed. I had been impressed by how hardworking he was.

He had that hippie look to him, though, which put up red flags for me. He had a long ponytail, and since he was an art teacher he wore clothes that were covered with paint all the time, and he smoked. He was not my idea of marriage material.

Eventually, we both could feel the strong attraction we had for each other. I think it was good that we were such good friends first. The years of flirting had proven that our attraction to each other was strong, but since we weren't dating we were able to talk to each other as friends and really get to know each other as people.

I slowly came around to considering him marriage material, after all. Yes, he had a ponytail, but he was very considerate and kind, not just to me but to everyone he encountered. Yes, he was a smoker, and I didn't like that, but it was so cute how he conscientiously put his cigarette out on the bottom of his shoe and put the butt in his pocket rather than litter. He really paid attention to me, to what I said and thought, and even quoted me to others.

Once we started dating, he wrote me songs, painted me pictures, wrote long love letters, made me dinner. I felt like I had found a prince of a man, only then I found out he didn't believe in marriage.

We were walking and debating one evening.

I told him, "I'm willing to let you go because of my strong conviction that marriage is the only way children should enter the world, based on my childhood."

I had told him many times that I could never put kids through the uncertainty of having parents who had not solidified their commitment to each other and to the family they were creating, legally. I believe that it was the fact that I accepted his position but was willing to stick by my own that ultimately led him to whisper in my ear that night:

"Lisa, you know what I think?"

I was expecting a list of reasons why living together was more real, more truthful. How every day you should prove your love by staying together and not rely on a marriage certificate.

Instead, he said, "I think we should get married."

I never once begged or badgered him. I simply listened to his point of view and was true enough to myself to tell him, "Living together's not good enough for me."

In the end, he decided he wanted to keep me, and he knew what it would take. We were married in New York in 1998 and now have two kids. He even cut his hair and stopped smoking—as wedding gifts to me. To this day, his family and friends speculate on what special tricks I used to change his views on marriage.

#13 AMANDA AND TONY

We were on the evening commuter train leaving Chicago when I first noticed my Tony. At the time, I was struggling to get through my senior year of art college by painting book covers for fellow students who were trying to sell their books and poems. However, looking at Tony who was sitting across the way from me, it seemed that he was in even worse shape then I was. He was wearing a jacket that was much too thin for a Chicago winter, and underneath it I could see he was just wearing a cotton undershirt. With him he carried a briefcase that looked like something out of an old movie. While he did look handsome, I remembered my mother telling me that it's rude to stare, so I busied myself organizing my art textbooks in my bag.

After I got off the train at the station near where I was living at the time, I went into the McDonald's that was nearby and ordered what was the highlight of my week: A Big Mac, fries, and a drink: my "luxury" meal. I had just sat down when I saw Tony come through the door. He went and ordered a to-go meal of three one-dollar sandwiches and a dollar drink before seeing me and then walking over. I was excited to see him but a little bit scared at the same time.

"Hello," he said, looking a bit bashful, as he seemed to be a bit humiliated to look trashy. "I saw you on the train."

"Really?" I was a bit excited that he had actually

seen me.

"Yeah," he said. "Listen, are you an artist?"

"Yes," I said.

"Well," Tony said, pulling out a business card, "my friend George and I are trying to get a decent color cover design for a comic book we're working on, but George hurt his hand this afternoon and can't hold a brush. Would you be interested in doing the cover for us? We can pay up to forty dollars but not a penny over it."

"Twenty-five is what I normally charge," I said, "and yes, I would be happy to paint it for you."

"All right," said Tony. "By the way, my name is Tony. Here's the specifics and my contact information." He handed me his card with a page of notes and then headed out the door.

I went home that night and drew and painted the cover for the comic. However, the place where George and Tony were living was very close to a nasty part of town. I didn't feel like going over there alone, so I had my sister's husband Brian, who's a policeman, drive me over to the apartment so that if anything went wrong, he would be able to protect me.

It turned out George and Tony were staying at a well-to-do apartment, not in that scary neighborhood at all, though when Tony answered the door, he made sure to shut it behind him.

"George is having a few friends over," he said. "Believe me, it wasn't my idea."

Tony's eyes were on Brian, and he stood up a little straighter than he had back at McDonald's. "But thanks for the painting."

"No problem," I said.

Still looking at Brian, Tony handed over my payment, which to my surprise was two twenties and a ticket to an art exhibit on Saturday.

I must have looked at the ticket too long.

"I thought you might like it," Tony told me, still looking at Brian, who smiled at him.

"Thanks," I said, though I didn't know how to tell him that my teacher had managed to get us into the museum for free the same day as the ticket. "Say, would you like to come with me to the museum?"

"Sure," Tony said, and then to Brian, "Is that OK with you?"

Brian let out the laugh he had been holding in the whole time. "It's OK, she's my sister-in-law!"

The museum was our first date. Tony showed he had a bit of an art background, and we had a very good time. However, as I was still in school and Tony was "living on hot air and hot dogs," our dates were still quite small until after graduation. I got an art teaching job at an elementary school in Virginia, and Tony managed to get a job writing history comics for a company over in England, though he was allowed to remain in the United States.

As the money started flowing in, we dated more and more until finally we were near our four year dating anniversary. Most of my girlfriends had married their boyfriends by then, and I was wondering why Tony was holding back on asking me to marry him.

One weekend in the summer, Tony and I went hiking in the mountains near my parents' house. As we sat down, I asked Tony about marriage. Tony told me that he had wanted to propose after our third date.

"I just don't want it to end because of my darling

family," he said.

I hadn't met any of Tony's family, but I knew he didn't like talking about any of them.

"What's wrong with them?" I asked.

"My mother's under the opinion that since I left school to go into the entertainment world, unlike my baby brother who just graduated in law, that any woman who marries me is to be looked down upon because of it."

"Well, Tony," I said, "I've got a thick skin, and besides, I have a feeling that if anyone were to say anything nasty to me, you would be more than willing to stand up for me."

"Yes," said Tony. "I would be willing to do that."

"And I would for you," I said.

"Well, that means a lot to me, Amanda," he said. "But you wouldn't mind a private wedding with just your family and a few of my friends?"

"If those are the only conditions, that's fine with me!" I said.

So the next day, Tony proposed, and in July of 2000 we tied the knot down in Mexico.

Tony's friend George, who had moved to Korea to work with an animation studio, paid for the wedding out of a gesture of friendship and for Tony

"Putting up with all my wild nights."

Ten years, three kids, and a dog later, we're still going strong.

#14 DEAN AND KAY HALLADAY

When I first met the man who would become my husband, I was already in a relationship but not a happy one. My then boyfriend was on several dating websites, and I caught him many times on my personal computer, scouring sites. So, in my attempt to finally catch him in the act, I created a fake profile on a dating website. To my surprise, one evening I got a message from a gentleman wanting to chat with me. I told him the story of why I was on the website and that my profile on the dating website was fake for that reason. He was so sympathetic and caring. We decided to meet and chat in person the next day over coffee. He could tell I was hurting over this other relationship and didn't push for anything more with me, but I really liked talking to him, and I was happily surprised to find someone who was so genuine.

After having coffee with the gentleman from the dating website, we talked on the phone for about a week. I then told him I needed a few days to myself and that I would call him when I could. Over the course of those few days, I broke up with the boyfriend who I couldn't trust. I took time to simply be alone and regroup. I didn't want the gentleman from the dating website to be a rebound relationship, but I couldn't stop thinking about him, so I got in touch with him and that is when Dean asked me on our first official date.

I knew my past relationships that started out too physical did not last long. I wanted to start off my relationship with Dean the right way, so before we went on our second date, I told him that I had not always done the right thing in relationships in the past and I wanted any relationships in the future to be different. I laid out my standards to him:

1) No sex before marriage.

2) We needed to attend church together.

3) We would commit our relationship to God.

To my surprise, he was impressed and happy with my standards and agreed to everything. After only a few months of dating, we just knew we were meant to be together. We started talking about marriage, but Dean had some concerns.

I had been in touch with my former boyfriend a few times because he had been calling me. I felt some lack of closure, even though I knew it was not the right relationship for me. Dean did not want to move forward in the relationship, especially proposing, unless I broke off all communication. After discussing it, I knew that in order to show respect to Dean and fully commit, ending all communication with my x-boyfriend would be necessary. I took the needed steps, including getting a new phone number in order to move on and wholly commit.

We went out to dinner on Valentine's Day and had a long three-hour wait for a table at a popular restaurant. While waiting, we walked around a local mall, and Dean pulled me into a jewelry store. I immediately panicked. I just wasn't prepared for the moment. He told me he just wanted to see what I liked, "just in case." It was fun to look at rings and try on some sparkly diamonds. I loved the princess cuts and how they looked on my finger. What I didn't know was how well Dean was taking notes during this brief shopping trip.

In late March, Dean was away on business in his family's home town. He told me he had a surprise for me, and he asked me to fly out for a long weekend to meet his parents for the first time. I really thought it was too soon for a proposal, so I kind of assumed he was going to tell me he shaved his goatee off or something silly like that, as Dean loved to surprise me. When I got on my connecting flight, I texted him to let him know I was turning off my phone. What I didn't know was that he had waited for that text so that he knew I couldn't be in contact with anyone, because he called my dad at that very moment and asked for my hand in marriage.

When I got off the plane and Dean picked me up, sure enough, he had shaved off his goatee! I laughed at him and thought I knew that was what his surprise was. He then took me to a quiet park where he said he'd always loved to go and watch the airplanes take off. We got out of the car, and he pointed to a huge DC-10 taking off. As I looked up, he got down on one knee. When I looked down, he was holding a sparkly princess cut diamond, and he asked me to marry him. I was in shock, but so happy. And I said yes! We were married 6 months later in 2004 and are to this day happily married with two boys, living in Indiana.

#15 ELODIE BROOKS

When I first met my future husband, he had been divorced for a year. He was still hurting from that process and only wanted to play the field. I thought he was very handsome, funny, and in general, a great guy, but I didn't think that this was the right time for us to date because I knew I wanted to be more than a rebound or a fling. Instead, we became great friends. We watched movies, hung out, even started a band. As I watched his line of girlfriends come in and out of his life, I was the one with the staying power.

Then one day I realized that I couldn't just be friends with him anymore. It was very difficult for me, but I told him that we had to "break up" because I wanted more than friendship, but I also didn't want to be one of his casual flings. After some good conversations, including discussing that I was waiting for marriage, he and I began to date in earnest.

And that was just the story of us dating!

Cue about a year, and our relationship was rock-solid. We were both moving along in our music careers, and I knew my feelings were very strong for him. He seemed like the man of my dreams, but he had dropped a few hints that marriage was not in his future. I understood to a degree: he'd been very hurt from his previous marriage, and at the end of the day, I think he was a little scared of getting hurt that way again.

On the one hand, no matter how many times I

explained that when I got married it would be forever, it didn't seem to be enough to convince him. On the other hand, I knew he was not a perpetual bachelor. He still talked about how much he loved being married and how much someday he wanted to be a great father with a big family. I knew it was in his heart that marriage would be in his future. He just had to know it, too.

However, I am not the kind of person who sits and waits for things to happen. While I wanted to marry him, I also was not interested in him taking forever to figure out what he already knew—that, of course, he loved me!

At one point, I brought up marriage. He immediately shied away from that discussion, but I flat-out said that if he asked me right then to marry him, I would say no. Well, that was a surprise to him. He immediately wanted to know why I would say that. I explained that I didn't think he was ready to ask someone to marry him and that he was still healing from his previous relationship. That knocked him for a loop!

Did I think that maybe if he wasn't certain of my feelings for him, that he would be even more interested in securing our relationship? Maybe! But, I was honest, too. At that point, I wouldn't have said yes if he had asked me. He wasn't ready yet. I also didn't say yes when he found out his job was taking him out-of-state.

When he told me the news, he looked like he was screwing up the courage to ask me to move with him there.

I flat-out said, "I hope you aren't thinking of asking me to move away with you!"

He again seemed a little surprised.

I explained I was not interested in moving out-of-state just to live with him and that I was very happy in my career as it was. I was only going to pick up and move away from my work for a husband—not a boyfriend. I explained that my parents were traditional and would be very unhappy if I moved in with someone. He respected that decision and said nothing more.

He wasn't scheduled to leave for his new job for a few months. This gave him plenty of time to plan an amazing proposal, and that time, I said yes! Afterward, he asked me if I had been serious when I said I wouldn't have married him if he'd asked me months before. I told him yes, but I explained that he had since made leaps and bounds by going to a counselor and discussing his fears and hopes with me. He had also been respectful of my personal boundaries, and I respected him for that. For those reasons, I told him yes. We've been married since the summer of 2012.

#16 MARISSA AND REIMUND

Well, I'm sure that if you ask my husband, he'll have a different version of this story than mine (and he is supposed to). We met at The Cheesecake Factory on Los Olas, and everything started there. I heard the familiar accent of German, and when I looked I saw that he was asking the restaurant hostess for directions. I also noticed that he was wonderfully handsome, dressed nicely, clean shaven, and had that European flare with manners that just set him apart from most men over here. I only tell you this so you know why I planned and plotted from that moment forward to marry him. The hostess could not understand a word he was saying, so I jumped in there—you know, to help!

Anyway, I gave him the directions that he was inquiring about—and my number... just in case he needed any more directions while he was here in the States. I later learned this is a common German thing: polite man that he is, Reimund then asked me to join him for coffee, as a thanks. I agreed, and we set a date for a few days later.

This is where my plotting really kicked into gear.

I knew he was returning to Germany soon. He knew that I lived with roommates, so when it came time to meet, I bent the truth a little. I told him one of them had just fallen and I needed to take him to the hospital, like the good roommate that I was. I asked Reimund if he would give me a rain-check. (My roomie had fallen, but there was no need for him to go to the hospital.)

Reimund was so cute with the rain-check, though: he said, "But it isn't raining?"

That kept the conversation going, and he called later to check on my wounded friend. He called a day later to see if I was free, and invited me to his condo for dinner and a swim.

This time, I went, and we ended up talking until 1 in the morning about previous relationships, family, work, and even our favorite foods. Major sparks were flying, and I knew that he was getting closer to exclusivity.

Instead of me just driving home, he volunteered to drive me because he got the idea that I was afraid of driving around at night by myself. (Not sure how he would have gotten that idea. Oh yeah: I fibbed. Just a little white lie though, right?) This way, he had to pick me up the next day so that I could pick up my car.

All too soon, it was time for him to go back to Germany. He said he was going to find someone to take care of the condo because he didn't know when he would be back.

His leaving was very sad for me, considering this was before Skype, so in order to keep in closer contact, I kinda fibbed again. I told him that my apartment building was about to be remodeled and I was having to move because I would not be able to afford the rent when the lease was up. Therefore, I could take care of his condo, that is, if he wanted me to.

He graciously said yes and that if he came back he would stay at a hotel so that I wouldn't need to worry about moving out.

So he left, and I felt like a princess in his castle by the sea. But, this princess was not going to wait forever for Prince Charming to come to his senses! I had to let him know that I was only here because of him. We wrote and called and became best friends with an ocean between us. I didn't have to pretend that we liked the same things; he was completing my sentences after six months of "long distance dating." We actually were meant to be together, and I knew it! So I had to do something drastic!

He was always saying that he never wanted to move to the USA, much less get married again. He had been married twice before, and each time it had been very short-lived, and the USA was nothing like Europe with all the different customs.

My mind started racing for a plan, and one was handed to me at a trip to my gynecologist, of all places.

I already knew he was protective of me with:

1) The ride home at night

2) Having me use his car because mine was a "death trap"

3) Him making sure that I was safe at his condo and not having to move out on my own.

I had never seen the blessing in my horrible cramps and bad periods until this day. My doctor told me that I should have a procedure called an endometrial ablation, a minor operation but with major pain. So I told him just a little about it.

"I have to have a procedure, nothing bad, but I may not be able to talk with you for a week or so."

He almost went insane with curiosity.

Two days before my appointment, he called from the airport for me to pick him up. I was shocked that it worked! He was here to nurse me back to health for a month and then had to return to Germany.

He stayed for the month of November, 2000.

On February 14, 2001, he flew back to the USA and asked me to marry him! We were married in May of 2001.

Since that time, he has received his green card and has been living here in the USA. Each year, we go to Germany to see his wonderful parents and visit the European culture and see the snow he misses from time to time. He is still the perfect man for me and says that I make him happier then he has ever been.

I do feel good in saying that I never really lied to him; I just didn't play fair. Yes, I played on his emotions and may have danced around reality, but he was and still is definitely worth it. Knowing his protective nature and making sure he knew that I needed him to take care of me from time to time helped him make the right decision... me.

#17 KYLIE AND COLE

I was married in 2012; I am still considered a newlywed. My husband Cole wasn't the easiest guy to catch. He is a US Marine and very true to it. It was a long grueling process to get him to settle down. We dated for 7 years before I finally got him to propose to me. He was previously married, and when we first became a couple he told me he never wanted to get married again. We were in love, and he knew it as did I, but he wasn't ready to admit it for a long time.

Even dating it was hard to make my husband commit. He wouldn't call me his girlfriend for a long time. He had the biggest commitment issues I had ever seen in a human being. When he asked me to be his girlfriend, I was surprised because I thought we would be "Just Friends" forever. He gave in when I stopped asking. He seems to do that a lot. After dating for many years, I felt like it would never become anything more, so I tried taking matters into my own hands.

I used to take him on dates to look at rings. He would get angry and walk away, telling me he would ask if and when he was ready. He told me all the time how he had a hard time trusting women after his first wife, but I didn't think it would be 7 years worth of a hard time! I would always make him watch wedding movies and look at wedding magazines with me. But because of his sour attitude, the more time I spent planning our future, the closer the end seemed. I was so worried about settling down that I wasn't even enjoying my time with him anymore.

I just wanted him to propose, already!

Six months into our relationship, I knew he was the one. It took me many years of convincing and eventually giving up, but he finally got down on one knee. I had begged and begged him to propose, for seven years. Year seven came around, and I had finally settled with the fact that we might only be "boyfriend and girlfriend" for the rest of my life. This wasn't what I wanted.

I told him, "I can't take this anymore. I'm going back home to my parents."

He pleaded for me to stay but still didn't want to get married.

"Kylie, I need you here with me. I love you. I love you so much."

"Then please, let's get married."

"I can't. Don't you understand? I just can't."

Although I knew I was being a sucker, I loved him. I decided to stay, but he still wanted to stay boyfriend and girlfriend, nothing more.

I told him, "I give up on marriage completely unless it's with someone else then because you're giving me no indication you want to be my husband."

Looking back, his mind must have started changing at this point. Once I had given up the idea of marriage, I started to distance myself and saw myself growing apart from him more and more every day.

He started to be nicer and nicer every day. It seemed that the more I pulled away, the more he pulled in. He asked how my day was when I got home, held doors open for me, and did all the little things he'd done when we first started dating but had slacked on until recently.

I wasn't ready to give up completely because I loved him so much, but enough is enough.

One day out of the blue, I told him, "It's either marriage or we're over," and at this point, I didn't think the first one was even an option.

When I was about to leave the whole relationship behind me, he popped the question. It was when I finally got over our marriage that he proposed. The actual proposal wasn't really what I was expecting.

It was pouring rain the Friday before Thanksgiving of 2011 in Southern California where we lived. We had spent all day looking for a new TV for his living room at his apartment. I was so exhausted and ready for bed. He looked at me after all day at the mall and other stores and said:

"Let's go to the beach."

I was so tired, I begged and pleaded, "Just take me home, please."

He kept insisting, "Let's go to the beach."

Finally, I gave in and said, "OK! Fine, let's go to the beach," tossing my hands in the air and rolling my eyes.

On the way, the rain got so heavy we had to pull off the road.

When we arrived at the beach, it was starting to ease up. We walked down onto the sand.

He tripped and fell on his face, filling up his cowboy boots with muddy water.

Already on the ground, he got up to one knee and gave me a spiel about how wonderful we are together.

Then he said those four little works I'd been

longing to hear for seven years.

"Kylie, will you marry me?"

My response was, "Wow, finally!"

We both laughed.

I was so happy to know I didn't have to keep trying over and over to convince him anymore. My man was tired of hearing me complain about marriage, so when I gave up he got down on one knee.

#18 JASON AND ANNA WALKER

Eight seconds doesn't seem very long, but it's all the time I needed to determine my future husband was out of his mind.

From my vantage point in the arena, I was trying to conduct a live radio broadcast and watch him at the same time. He was on the back of a raging bull, and the second hand of the clock seemed to be stuck. The words that formed in my mind never made it from my lips as I watched him fall and the bull spin and drop its head for a charge. Jason tried to roll from the bull's path, but it was too late, and I watched in stunned horror as the bull drove Jason's body into the mud. He lay motionless, his body at a peculiar angle—I thought I was looking at a dead man. The bull spun and charged back toward the chutes, and two rescue men ran to aid the fallen bull rider. The arena went deadly quiet as the men worked to bring the rider back to his feet, and then it exploded into thunderous applause as the injured man waved his hand, leaning heavily on the men at his sides.

As the rodeo proceeded, I glanced over my shoulder several times, hoping to catch sight of the rescue men and get an update on the injured rider. Finally, toward the close of the day's events, the announcer gave a small update. The rider was fine, but he had been transported to a nearby hospital. I phoned my boss and told him I'd be gone the rest of the day. I wanted to check on what should have been a dead man.

Across town, the hospital was a buzz of reporters. The rider was a local favorite, and all were scrambling for the best byline in the evening news.

Knowing I had little chance of bypassing the swarm, I decided to enter through the emergency room entrance.

At the door, a concerned nurse stopped and asked, "What's your business, Ma'am?"

With a straight face, I said, "Will you escort me to my brother, the famous bull rider?"

Whom I'd never met in my life.

By this time, Jason had been moved to a private room.

My hands were shaking when the nurse brought me close to his door. Knowing the man inside would not recognize me; I stopped her just short of the knob and said, "Maybe I should go in alone; he's probably seen enough people in uniform for one day."

She smiled, and as she walked away, I opened the door and peeked inside.

The rider was in sorry shape to say the least, with one arm in a cast and his ribs wrapped tightly. His face looked swollen and purple in places, and one eye was bandaged. As he looked up at me, I just shook my head and then asked the one question that had been on my mind since the second he'd fallen.

"What were you thinking?"

With a sideways grin, the injured cowboy shook his head and said, "Ma'am, there ain't much thought goes into bull riding."

After he was released from the hospital, I learned that there was more to Jason Walker than just guts and a thick skull.

Over the next several weeks, we dated as our schedules allowed, and realized we really weren't all that different, at least as far as what drove us each to pursue the career we'd chosen was concerned.

Jason loved the danger, the adrenalin rush, and the pure exhilaration of being completely on his own. On the back of an angry bull, it's all on you. Whatever happens is determined solely by you and your actions.

Radio is very similar: the minute the microphone is turned on, all the preparation and training in the world won't help you if you make a split-second bad decision. There is no room for error. Radio is demanding, requires a full time commitment, and leaves very little room for home and family.

Bull riding and radio require very much the same self reliance. Jason and I had both been married before, and our careers had slowly destroyed the marriages. Over time, he'd come to the conclusion that marriage and a family simply weren't in the cards. But, as more time went by, we slowly realized we were completely accepting of each other's professional lives. There was never any argument about one of us being late, out of town, or placing ourselves into danger.

As our time together increased, so did the desire for each other. Many nights, Jason would leave my apartment because he knew if he stayed, we'd take our relationship to a higher level. His fear of commitment and possible failure always stopped him just short of taking action. Our fist real argument ensued shortly.

It was late, snow was falling, and Jason saw no reason for me to drive home.

It hit me then: our relationship was impossibly

deadlocked. Jason wasn't going to fall to his knees and ask me to marry him. I wasn't going to settle for anything less. Anger and an overwhelming feeling of hopelessness washed over me as tears welled.

I stood to leave, and I told him, "I won't be coming back."

He stood and demanded, "Oh, no, you're not leaving without an explanation."

Through tears, I told him, "I love you, but this isn't enough for me. I see you risk your life every single time you ride, no fear, no hesitation. But the thought of spending your life with me scares you so badly you won't even consider the thought!"

Jason wrapped his arms around me and then whispered, "Spending my life with you isn't what scares me. I don't want to rope you into something. But if you try to walk out that door, I'll hog tie you, Girl."

Looking up into his eyes, I saw nothing but sincerity. "Maybe I want to be roped in," I said, with a grin.

Jason's laugh was contagious, and I couldn't help but chuckle as he slid to one knee in front of me. "I don't have my rope handy, but maybe this will hold you," he said, as he pulled a ring from his pocket.

On January 14, 1991, I became Mrs. Anna Walker, and Jason and I just celebrated our twenty-second wedding anniversary.

#19 RENEE AND DAVID

The moment in time when I realized I'd met the perfect soul mate was in the year 2009. The seven years prior had been difficult, to say the least. I was a single mother who was only interested in raising my young daughter and working. The hours in between were spent with church service and an exercise regime to regain my physical strength. I had prayed for the Lord to guide me on my next relationship as I had my little girl as my number one focus. My heart had been crushed, and as far as I was concerned I would rather be single than go through that again.

In December of 2008, a friend approached me about a man she worked with who was, in her words, "a real prince."

I had been alone for so long, and my daughter was growing up. I felt a whisper to give a date a try. I told my friend to go ahead and give this prince my phone number so that he could contact me to arrange a meeting.

I was not going to introduce a stranger to my baby girl right off the bat, so when he called, we agreed to meet in a public place. I was thinking of safety first, and did not want him to know where I lived. Atlanta, Georgia can be cold in the winter, but you never know what the weather is going to be like. We agreed to meet at a restaurant. The day was crisp and cloudy with a chance for rain or snow.

I walked into Chili's and saw a handsome man

sitting to my right. I didn't want to assume, so I went up to the desk, and he approached me. I was so nervous, but when I looked into his bright blue eyes the kindness I saw there touched my heart immediately.

We were seated, and we had lunch. We discussed our lives, both having been divorced. His divorce was much more complicated than mine. He had two teenagers and one very disgruntled ex-wife. Mine was more amicable, for we had both moved on peacefully, with our daughter's best interests in mind. He disclosed some financial issues he had right away, not wanting to move forward without me knowing about his past. I had similar financial issues, but we both had learned from those mistakes. We ended the delightful lunch with a walk at a nearby nature preserve. The day was perfect. When we returned to my car, he asked me out on another date, and I jumped with a yes.

Over the course of a few dates, I prayed to the Lord for His guidance. I was feeling things in my heart that I had long suppressed in a need to stay grounded for my daughter's sake. By the third date, I already knew in my heart of hearts that I wanted to marry David. We had an instant chemistry, and the physical attraction was strong.

His son was fine with the relationship, but his teenage daughter was still having trouble with her father's divorce from her mother three years prior. David and I discussed marriage, but because of his daughter's misgivings, deciding when we would actually go through with it was difficult.

I had introduced him to my daughter only after I was totally sure of our future together. A small amount of investigation work was done just to make sure he had no evil skeletons lurking in the background. Everyone who knew him said he was the nicest man on the planet. The whisper I kept hearing was telling me he was the one. Over the course of the next couple of months, our relationship was solid.

We discussed the problem with his daughter not approving, and I helped him realize that she might never approve, due to her mother constantly causing issues for him anywhere she could. I helped him see that I would be strong enough to deal with any issues we would face with his ex-wife and children. My daughter loves his children and vice-versa. We talked about taking baby steps with his daughter, but that we would continue on with plans to marry and deal with any issues that might arise afterward.

We prayed for God's guidance on the situation and proceeded to set the date of September 26, 2009. Because of our Christian background and sharing of faith, we sought out a minister. We had to take classes, just as a younger couple would. It was fun to go through the classes even though we both were older adults with children.

Unfortunately, his daughter was so upset via her mother's help that she did not participate in the wedding. It is a difficult situation when there is a bitter party who uses the children as a weapon against the other parent. Later, his daughter would disclose to us that she was afraid to be in the wedding for what her mother would think. David's son stood up for him, and my daughter for me. It was a beautiful wedding, surrounded by loved ones and friends all praying for our happiness.

The Bible says divorce and remarriage is adultery, and we both struggled with that issue. David even asked the preacher about it, and we summed it up as sin in our lives. We also believe that we can be forgiven for our sins, and we prayed for forgiveness and for blessings on our union.

Now that we are happily married, we are

convinced that God was indeed working to put us together. The road has not been all roses, and yet we work together to build a relationship that can stand up to those tests that come our way. Our physical attraction to each other, as well as our mental attraction, was too strong to deny. When two people care about each other in such a way it is necessary to marry. The ability to be a good example to our children through marriage was the only solution. We strongly believe that God blessed us with each other for our faithfulness to Him and our children. When we sought answers for our attraction and dilemma over the children, marriage was the only answer.

It is rare to find an actual soul mate in this world, but when I spoke the words,

"I, Renee, take thee, David, to be my lawfully wedded husband,"

I felt the approval of God shining down on us. We have been blessed with our union and the children have blossomed with our devotion to each other.

#20 ASHLEE AND JAMES

For years, James refused! I couldn't get him to even speak of marriage until something dreadful happened four years into our relationship. Before that, we would joke about it. But four years of being madly in love with a gorgeous blond guitarist was getting the better of me, and I didn't know if he wanted to get married, have children, or live a lifetime with me.

After a while of thinking of marriage, I started to mention it here and there. Subtle hints would be dropped.

"I bet this place throws a great reception."

He'd cringe and back away like a frightened child.

I never knew for so long why he felt that way. He wouldn't tell me. It got to the point where we'd fight about marriage and why I felt like it'd never happen. I didn't get any why-not out of him until a month before the accident.

We were in a massive fight one night after we went to dinner. I'd watched a man propose to the woman he loved at another table. The entire restaurant smiled and congratulated them. She looked so happy, smiling from ear to ear. In the mirror of the restroom after excusing myself, I found myself looking the complete opposite. I didn't want to fight him, so I avoided crying about not getting married in front of him. He noticed though and said nothing.

After we made it to my house, I was the one who blew up at him.

"Do you love me at all?" I yelled as continuous tears fell.

His eyes went from wide with shock to wild with anger.

"Ashlee, I'm not getting married." He tried to end the conversation.

"Why not? I have loved you for four years unconditionally, and never once have you said anything about loving me—not just like that, but for the rest of our lives!"

"I live in the moment."

"That's a lie!" I finally shouted, calling him out.

He looked at me with anger, but dropped that anger quickly.

"It's all a lie, James! You're scared of something, and I don't know why! You don't tell me anything! I watched a happy couple get engaged tonight. A year or so from now, they'll be happily married, and we won't! Why?"

I was screaming now.

I plopped onto my couch, defeated, and sighing in that defeat.

He just stood there looking just as defeated as I was.

I didn't expect answers anymore. I had given up.

But James finally gave me the answers I had sought after for years.

"When we were in high school, you would ask how I got a black eye or a broken wrist, remember?"

I looked up at him and nodded, staring at him in shock as his words unfolded mysteries about him I never knew.

"Well, my father was abusive. Not really toward me, but toward my mother. All the injuries I'd get were from defending her. I'd gotten tall enough to go against him, but that didn't stop him from giving her a bloody lip or punching me in the face for trying to stop it. It went on for years, and then I learned that my father started getting that way when he married her. Right after he married her, actually."

I continued staring at him even when his eyes were facing the ground in shame.

"Do you think that you'll get that way if we get married?" I asked him, incredulous.

He nodded as he pinched the bridge of his nose and walked to the window.

"James, you're not your father. I've met your father five times, and with each visit I disliked him more, but you are not that man. You may look like him on the outside, but you don't look like him on the inside, Love."

James sighed and stepped away from the window, moving toward the door.

"I need some time, Ash. I'll call you."

And just like that, he was out the door.

I didn't see him for a month.

I spent many nights crying and feeling sorry for myself. My friends were supportive and helpful, but after a while they started suggesting we go out and try to have fun. So, finally, I agreed. They all silenced their phones and told me to, also. I'd spent weeks waiting for his call without getting it, so I figured a few hours wouldn't hurt.

Lynn and Sophie were taking me to see my favorite band in concert, but the drive was going to take about two and a half hours. Lynn was driving, and Sophie was in the back seat with me, making me laugh with old pictures of herself that she had taken at a convention when she dressed up like Velma from Scooby-Doo. I was there in the pictures, too, dressed up as cat-version of Scooby. It had been a stupid idea now that I saw the pictures, but I'd been fourteen at the time. Anyway, now it was fun to laugh at the pictures.

Almost two hours into the drive, Lynn popped in an old CD containing a play list of songs we had listened to often when we were younger. I was masking my pain with fake happiness and singing to a random song when we were hit by another driver, causing the other car to flip and causing us to drive off-course and into a ditch. I didn't wake up until I was at the hospital.

My injuries were minor, as were Lynn's and Sophie's. No one got seriously hurt, but James was so worried about me he stayed at my bedside the entire time. He refused to sleep until I opened my eyes. The doctors told him I'd be fine, but he wouldn't hear it. Typical James.

After I opened my eyes, he smiled and grabbed my hand.

"You didn't answer your phone," he said.

"You finally called, huh? I put my phone on silent, because Sophie and Lynn were taking me to a concert."

He smirked at me and kissed me.

"Ashlee, I love you. And I want you to marry me."

My eyes widened massively. I didn't know what to even say besides an automatic "yes."

We both laughed, and he hugged me, but tears fell anyway.

At first, I thought it had taken the accident to get his attention, but it turned out he'd spent a month thinking about the words I'd said to him:

"You're not your father."

When he'd started thinking clearly, he'd given me a call. I listened to the voice mail after his proposal, and it was beyond romantic:

"Ashlee, I need you. I don't want to spend any more of my life without you. Please call me back."

I could tell he'd been crying.

We were married in 2011 in a beautiful church that was decorated in white lilies and lace.

#21 JERRIE RUSSENBERGER

After being widowed and then single for seventeen years, I was finally ready to settle down again. I started looking for someone who also wanted to settle down. When I finally found the man I thought I could live the rest of my life with, guess what? He did not want to get married.

We'd been together four years, and we enjoyed each other's company, but he kept on saying:

"I do not want to get married."

I would pretend to agree with him, "Yeah, I don't, either," when on the inside I really did want to.

Sometimes, I would tell him, "I'm going to break up with you and find someone who does want to get married." Believe me, that did not work.

He would always reply, "Just go right ahead."

He had been married once before, and it had not ended on a good note, which most divorces don't. He had been married for 27 years to the same woman when she had an affair, so he had decided that he did not want to ever go through that again.

I had also been married before, but my previous marriage had ended when my husband died, so I had a totally different view on marriage. I knew marriage could be good.

I had to make a plan, or else I was going to have to decide whether or not I wanted to stay in a relationship that was never going to be a marriage. For me, it was now or move on, and I really wanted it to be now. I did not want to put the time or effort into a relationship that was not going to be a marriage.

I figured I had to show him that marriage could be good and could last, if it was between the right man and woman. So I started thinking, "What could I do that would make him want to get married?"

My first thought was to take him to a friend's anniversary party. They had been married 43 years. We had a good time at the anniversary party, but it still did not make him ready.

I had friends who had been married for a long time, and I had friends that had been married for a short time. I decided it was time to surround ourselves with these friends. I would subtly ask questions about how they met and how long had they been married. They looked at me kind of like I was off my rocker because I already knew the answers to the questions I had asked. That really didn't seem to be pushing him any closer to the idea of marriage.

I thought, "I would stand a chance if I could only get him to consider the idea of getting married instead of an emphatic 'No!' every time I bring the subject up!"

Then we started attending church together.

At first, the church was held in a bar, so it didn't bother him, attending that church. The church membership grew so much that they moved into a regular church. It included more activities for couples to do things together, and we attended several weddings of couples who attended church with us. I had stopped even mentioning marriage.

I started back to college and was so busy I actually enjoyed the days we didn't spend together.

Then one day we attended another wedding held at our church, and he brought up the subject.

"Are you still thinking about marriage?"

I just replied, "I'm enjoying going back to school," and I talked about all of the people I had met and how I liked my life just like it was. Then I let it drop.

A few weeks later, he brought it up again.

"We could wake up next to each other and eat breakfast together and plan our lives together if we had the same roof over our heads."

I thought he was talking about just living together.

I point blank told him, "I have no desire to give up my place to just live with you. If we lived together, it would be because we were married."

To which he replied, "Duh! What do you think I was talking about?"

Only later did I find out that he was afraid he was going to lose me after I went back to school. He said that I was always busy and did not spend as much time with him as I used to.

So we got married on July 27, 2007, on the day we had met four years prior.

#22 MAYA AND JASON

The first time I met my future husband, he was lying on a friend's couch, snuggled up on a cold January day in a fuzzy brown blanket, just his toes and bright blue eyes showing. I was friends with his brother, who had said to me with a wink and a nudge:

"You gotta meet my brother."

I was finishing my senior year of college. Jason had just returned from a two-year Mormon mission, and I just wasn't ready to get serious with anyone, much less the guy in the fuzzy blanket with the bright blue eyes.

But oh, those blue eyes!

And, when he finally stuck his head out from under that blanket like an agile turtle peeking out of its shell, it turned out that he had beautifully white teeth that dazzled in a magnificent smile.

I sat down on the couch and watched a basketball game with him, his brother, and my good friend Lisa. I actually enjoyed it, his feet every now and then "accidentally" touching my leg, sending shots of electricity through my body. That's how interested in this bright-eyed, fabulous smile guy I was: I actually volunteered to watch a basketball game.

He turned out to be very good company, indeed.

I was a musical theatre major finishing up my Bachelor's Degree, and he had a full-time job, but he managed to find time to come and see my shows (and then sing along with the CDs for years afterward).

One beautiful, warm spring night after a show, we were walking around campus. The stars were blazing in the cobalt sky, and we were laughing and singing songs from the show. He took me in an awkward dance position, placing one hand on my lower back and the other meeting mine in a simple, elegant pose (he never was much of a dancer). He sweetly asked me to teach him how to waltz. He was biting his lip a little, a sign of nervousness I'd learned, and we put our arms around each other and waltzed awkwardly while joyfully laughing all the while under the beautiful night sky.

I taught him the *Fiddler on the Roof* song, "Do You Love Me?" It's a goofy duet about a couple who have been in an arranged marriage for twenty-five years, and we would lie on top of the covers in the summer heat, singing in our silliest voices. I was hooked. He had lived for two years in the south of France, so he spoke beautiful French. I had studied French in college to achieve my BA, and though mine was not nearly as fluent as his, we would have long conversations in French. I had fantasies about us getting married, living a long, amazing life in New York City—where, of course, I would be a Broadway star—and then retiring to our little cottage overlooking a vineyard in the South of France.

After being together with him for a few months, and much to my own surprise, I told Jason that I wanted to get married.

But he hesitated. He said that he had too many friends break-up and too many family members who had been through divorces. He essentially shrugged his shoulders and inferred:

"If it ain't broke, why fix it?"

Since the relationship was relatively new, I decided to give him the benefit of the doubt, but I was getting increasingly ready for the relationship to move forward on a significant level. I thought about perhaps living together, then considered our religiously conservative families. If I wanted to be with Jason, I would have to wait.

About a year and a half into our relationship, Shanny, a good mutual friend of ours who had been recently married, drove more than two hours to see me in a show. I was so honored that she had come to see me, and I had hoped to catch up with her, but unfortunately I had previous commitments and was not able to spend time with her after the show.

Early the next morning, my telephone rang.

Rubbing the sleep out of my eyes, I said, "Hello?"

It was my friend, Lisa, whose voice was thick with tears. "Shanny," she sobbed into the phone. "Shanny was killed in a car accident last night on the way home from your show."

I held the phone to my ear but could not find any words. I stared in disbelief at the blanket I was sitting on, listening with shock and disbelief to my friend sob and sob.

A few days later, Lisa, Jason and I piled uncomfortably into a small car I had borrowed from my mother to make the long drive to Shanny's funeral. Her husband of fewer than nine months, now a widower, sat in the front row of the church, his body heaving with grief and tears. We listened to wonderful stories about how this young girl, not even 21 yet, had been robbed of her bright and promising life because of a horrible mistake made by another driver. We were in disbelief, as were the hundreds of others who had turned out to pay their respects.

After the funeral, we all returned to the car, but Lisa went to say goodbye to another friend, leaving Jason and me alone. Though not very often openly demonstrative, he was quietly crying in the backseat of the car. My eyes met his in the rear view mirror.

He said in almost a whisper, "I don't want to lose you like Joe lost Shanny. I don't want my life to pass me by without you in it because I was too afraid of breaking up or getting a divorce."

My own eyes, bright green to his blue, started to blur with tears.

"Maya, will you marry me?"

I turned to face him, our cheeks touching, wet with tears.

"Yes!" I happily cried. "Of course I will!"

At just that moment, Lisa opened the car door with a quizzical look on her face.

"What's going on in here?"

Jason and I just laughed.

We got married in May of 1999. A lot of things have changed, but I will tell you one thing that remains the same: we still sing that goofy song together.

#23 MEGAN AND ALEX

I was in my junior year at the University of California at Northridge, working on my bachelor's degree in philosophy. He was a full-time logistics worker in LA. We met one desperate day during my search for one last roommate to move in before school started in the fall. A mutual friend introduced us, and as crazy as it sounds, from the first time I met him, shook his hand, and looked into his eyes, I knew that Alex was going to be a very important person to me.

Alex did not move in with me that fall; I found a female roommate instead, something he and I were both pleased with. I didn't know if I could live with a guy, and he didn't want to be trapped in a house as the only guy with three other girls.

We started talking and flirting in August of 2005. He was sweet, funny, intelligent, hard-working, handsome, confident, generous, and caring. We went to dinners and movies and lakes and beaches, and I was in love. Our conversations would last for hours, and I could talk to him about anything. We argued about politics; he's ultra conservative, and I'm the opposite. We complained together about our troubles and hardships and gave each other strength when we feared we couldn't cope with growing up.

I remember once coming back to school after visiting my father's house. I collapsed into his lap and cried.

He held me, kissed my forehead, and said:

"Megan, I don't know what happened at home, but I want you to know that I love you, and I'll always be here to be your hero."

He held me until I fell asleep, puffy faced and still sniffling.

My grandmother was in the hospital and probably wouldn't make it another week. He came with me to the hospital every day to visit her and cried with me the day we had to let her go. It was that day that I decided I never wanted to let him go.

Alex and I had been together 10 months when we both started shyly bringing up our future together. He would tell me about his dreams of starting a business and joke about how good my cooking was going to taste after he came home from his long days of working. We would talk about the color of our kitchen and what kind of parents we'd be, but we never directly talked about getting married. I knew he wasn't ready to settle down, and I was still trying to finish school, but I knew marriage was what I eventually wanted.

After two and a half years together, we had been through one graduation, two job changes, countless struggles and fights and make-ups, three different apartments, a dog, two fish, and more energy than I ever thought I had in me. We had stable jobs, an apartment together, and a wonderful outlook on our future. I was ready to settle down, but I could tell Alex was still hesitant. I guessed he didn't think he was ready for stay-at-home life. He wanted to have fun and travel and do something crazy.

We needed a way to get the rest of the restless out of him so that we could start our life together.

I had an idea, but I wasn't sure if it would work.

I decided that for our three-year anniversary I was going to surprise Alex with a 3,000 mile road trip across the country to visit his cousin in Maine. It was something he had been talking about doing for years.

Over the next six months, I put any extra money I had in a savings account for the trip.

I told Alex, "I want to do something special for our anniversary," but I didn't tell him what.

He and I both took two weeks off work and waited what seemed like an eternity for the day of our anniversary to come. He begged and pleaded for me to tell him what his surprise was, but I refused.

After extensive planning, secret-keeping, and money-saving, it was finally September 18, our anniversary. I had packed the bags the night before and awoke to Alex's anxious questioning as to where we were headed.

I told him, "We're going on a road trip—to see Chris!"

"Don't joke with me!"

"Really! I have the money saved up for gas and motels, and Chris is expecting us! Happy anniversary!"

He laughed for a minute and hugged me tight.

"This means the world to me. I am so excited to go on this adventure with you!"

We stopped in several states on the way to Maine. We spent a night in Salt Lake City, two nights in Denver, one night in a little town in Nebraska that I can't remember the name of, one night in Buffalo, and one night in Plattsburgh. We also saw a bunch of little towns along the way. It was the scariest, most invigorating adventure of my life. We had some problems along the way like getting lost, our car breaking down, food poisoning, and losing money, but we worked together to overcome every obstacle that was thrown in our way. We met so many wonderful people along the way and became closer as a couple in that short period of time than we had in three years.

It was just the medicine he needed.

I didn't even need to bring up marriage.

Two weeks after we got back home, Alex took me on a surprise trip to Disneyland. At the end of the night, right before we were about to leave the park, he took me to the castle and got down on one knee.

"The road trip we took together showed me that you are everything I ever needed. Megan, will you marry me?"

"Yes!"

We were married 5 months later. Our ceremony was a small gathering, just close friends and family. We became husband and wife March 5, 2005 on the beach at sunset. It was everything I ever wanted.

#24 STAN AND TRACY MITCHUM

Stan and I were friends long before we started dating. We met at a restaurant supply company where we both worked. He was in the engineering department, and I was a project manager, so we worked closely on designing commercial kitchens. From the start, I loved his outgoing, comical personality. He was always playing practical jokes and kidding around, and it made the day go by faster.

As co-workers often do, over time I found out that he was going through a divorce. I had just gotten out of a long-term relationship, so we began sharing stories with each other that created a bond. We would often hang out after work at a local park to talk, or meet for dinner. All as friends. I don't think the idea of us dating entered our minds until probably a year or so after we became close. Neither of us was ready for a serious relationship at the time because we both had been hurt in the past.

One Friday night while we were having dinner at our favorite restaurant downtown, he asked me if I would like to go on an official date. I was shocked and told him that I would have to think about it and let him know in a couple of days. I made sure that he knew that I wasn't rejecting him; I just had to think seriously about my decision. We both had children from our previous marriages, and I wanted to consider how a new relationship might affect my two daughters.

Plus, I was worried. If things went sour, then I would lose my best friend.

I called my best girlfriend and asked her opinion.

She said, "What are you so afraid of? Your relationship isn't really going to change. You two have already been dating! You're just both so worried about your past mistakes that you're afraid to venture out into a new relationship that would probably be amazing because you have so much in common."

I called him back on Monday and set up a date for the next Friday night, but it wasn't all smooth sailing from there.

After dating for about three years, I was ready to settle down and get married.

We spent our weekends together and talked every day. I had left the company and started a different job once we started seeing each other, so we wouldn't have a conflict of interest at work. We had moved into the same apartment complex in two separate apartments so we could be closer to each other, and his son and my daughters got along great.

There shouldn't have been any problems, but there was one: he just wasn't ready to remarry. His wife had really hurt him when she asked for a divorce, and he didn't want to risk going through that pain again.

We had a heart-to-heart talk about our future.

I said, "When are we going to get married and combine our families and settle down?"

He said, "I'm not sure that I'll ever want to marry again. I love you, and you are my best friend, so I feel like I have to be as honest as possible."

I was devastated! I had been secretly planning our wedding in my head for months and felt sure he was going to propose any day. I didn't handle this news well at all.

I said, "I think it would be better if we spent some time away from each other."

The girls and I left that weekend, I was so upset, and went to visit their uncle, my brother, in another state. While we were gone, I didn't return Stan's phone calls or emails. I wanted to punish him for what I felt was him wasting my time and hurting my feelings.

After the girls went to bed, my brother and I had a difficult conversation, and he asked me:

"Can you see yourself with anyone else?"

I truly couldn't.

Every time I envisioned my future, it included my best friend. I knew then that I had overreacted to his honesty and needed to have a serious conversation.

As soon as we returned home, I suggested we drop the kids off at a movie so we could talk. Once the two of us were alone, I took a deep breath and then opened my heart.

"I appreciate you not leading me on with false promises. I cannot imagine living my life without you in it. I promise I am OK with our relationship continuing the way it is, and I won't pressure you any more about marriage."

We hugged, cried, and went to pick the kids up.

Six months later, we were at our favorite Mexican restaurant when the mariachi band stopped by our table and started a Spanish love song.

He slid out of his seat, dropped down on one knee, and proposed!

I was overwhelmed, and I cried! I couldn't believe this was happening.

He said, "I'm finally ready. Thank you for not

pressuring me and waiting patiently. I want to spend the rest of my life with you."

We were married on July 3rd, 2010 at a ceremony on the lake with fireworks at the end, with all of our friends and family gathered around to wish us well. I'm so glad that I didn't pressure or try to trick him into something that he wasn't ready for. I know that he made a decision that was all his, on his schedule, and I love him all the more for it.

#25 STEPHENIE ALEXIS HARTFORD

I will never forget the day I asked him if we would ever get married. We were sitting on the front porch waiting for his brother, and somehow the marriage conversation popped up.

"Could you ever see yourself married to me?"

As soon as I asked the question, his eyes got big, and he turned his head towards the tree line. When he turned back to face me, he explained.

"Marriage is nothing but a label slapped on a relationship."

I was instantly crushed.

I had known him for years and always pictured him to be the marriage type, but apparently I was off by millions of miles. It was like pulling a tooth to even get him on the topic after I brought it up the first time. I felt like I was almost forcing him to even get the word "marriage" out of his mouth.

The only related thing he would say was:

"Well, when the ring hits the finger, manhood goes out the window."

I hated it when he said that. Half the time, to bring it up I would talk about friends of ours getting married, in hopes to pressure him into proposing. The other times I was blunt about the subject and wound up hurting myself, which was most definitely not worth the battle.

As a little girl and even as an adult, I had done the cliché planning of my dream wedding, so when he murmured those words, they cut right through my dreams. I just didn't see how he considered it to be a label. Marriage is about commitment, true love, longevity and loving each other to your last dying breath. But apparently we had extremely different opinions on that subject.

I never brought the topic up again until we had been in a full blown, committed relationship for two years. When I brought it up for the second time, he basically just smiled and repeated the same words he'd said years before:

"Well, when the ring hits the finger, manhood goes out the window."

I just didn't get it. I was horribly confused and hurt. I felt like it was just an excuse not to get married to me. I knew he saw how much it hurt me because the pain could not be hidden in my eyes.

The one thing he had never wanted to do was hurt me. He hated seeing any bit of sadness in my eyes. He would do anything to avoid it. And avoid it he did.

After having his words hurt me for a second time, I decided against ever bringing it up again. It was too much on my pride and self-esteem. I just wished he would change his mind. Six months went by, and still I felt distance between us when we laid down in bed every night. All I wanted was to be married to the love of my life. Was that too much to ask? It was not that I thought he didn't love me. I just thought he didn't love me enough.

But, I was wrong.

In spring of 2004, my husband proposed to me at my parents' farm. We were at a family barbecue when he knelt on one knee and held out a ring in front of my entire family. The shock was so intense that I could not control my tears. I was so happy and in love, and most of all, shocked. I guess my times of badgering and crying finally paid off.

The week after the proposal, I started planning out our wedding and writing my soon to be new name repeatedly on paper. Stephenie Alexis Hartford had never sounded so sweet and elegant. After months of planning, our big day came in August 2004. The wedding was filled with loving family members and friends, pink and white flowers and surrounded by the family farm. I remember feeling so happy that I cried every time I pictured him slipping the ring on my finger. I never thought I would be able to marry the man of my dreams, the one I would lay down my entire life for.

I really think if I had kept begging my husband about getting married that we would never have gotten to that special day.

Although he was appalled by the thought of putting a ring on my finger at first, he saw how it hurt me when he said no. He told me much later that just my pained reaction to his words had been enough to send him to the jewelry store to buy me a ring.

It is funny how I thought his love for me was untrue. In all reality, he loved me so much that he did something he absolutely did not want to do, just to put a smile on my face.

I used to think that he only bought the ring to shut me up about weddings and our friends' engagements, but deep down I now know that all he wanted was to make me happy, and if it meant throwing a ring on my finger he'd do it. Out of all the men I've known and met briefly, I do honestly believe my husband is one of the select few who throw away their pride just to bring a little joy into their woman's life.

#26 AUBREY AND LARRY

New York is hot in June, even in the suburbs. Meeting someone online can be dangerous. I had a lot of help, since I cleaned houses for the local police. Background checks made easy! I met him June 7, 2009. I didn't believe in soul mates. They just seemed like something in fairy tales, but little did I know my true love story was just beginning...

On a Christian dating site, I met Larry, and we were up for a week straight, talking endlessly. I had never felt such a connection to anyone before, and neither had he. Although I was looking for a husband, I didn't want to broadcast it and scare him away! I decided to play it smart and take it slow... very slow. However, life being what it is, he bought me a plane ticket after asking:

"How long will it take before you'll come out here?"

"Well, send me a ticket and I'll come!"

So, I flew out to Montana to see him one week after we "met."

The mountains were magnificent, just where I always wanted to be. It was a dream come true and many, many prayers answered. I had given up on my dreams a while ago and stopped praying for a way out of the city. I guess it is true that when you are at the very bottom there is no way out but up. I had reached what I thought was the bottom a few years earlier, but soon found out there is always a way to get down even lower.

We spent two weeks together in gorgeous blue and green Montana, and then I returned to my bleak existence amid concrete and steel. We had decided that I would move out a couple weeks later, so I had a lot of packing to do! In an amazing turn of events, I found a renter to take my house, a teacher to take my violin students, and a cleaning lady to accept all of my appointments! There was no doubt this was meant to be. We both knew we were blessed by God. We knew we were soul mates.

I moved out on the condition that we would be husband and wife, and since times were tough financially, we moved into an apartment together for what I thought would be a short time. It took some time to find a good job, and I kept wondering when the big day would be. Knowing that nagging is never good, I waited and waited. Of course, I hinted and hinted as well!

Larry's first excuse for not rushing into marriage was that it was now a government operation and the church no longer legally supervised it.

I could see his point, since you can claim yourself "legally married" just by filing taxes together (which we did)! However, I pleaded with him to just get it over with for my sake. I needed a real wedding and a real dress.

Next, he told me that God had put us together and he knew we would be together forever, so it counted in God's eyes as a marriage.

Granted, we *had* exchanged vows of some sort to each other, but I felt that was simply an expression of feelings and not a sacred promise.

This excuse making went on for some time.

Many arguments and wondering-why's later, I

finally suggested Las Vegas: cheap, effective, quick, and no one had to be invited!

He went for it!

I picked out the dress, shoes, veil, flowers, chapel—and practiced my walk. We went down to get a 12-12-12 wedding date! The last time it would be available for quite some time!

After the five-minute ceremony and pictures, I asked him, "So? How was it?"

"Well, it's over, and I hope you're happy 'cause I'll never do it again."

"And you'll never have to, 'cause these shoes are too tight, and I will never wear them again!"

So now I could stop wondering and just relax...

#27 RAYA AND JOSE

I had been pretty wild in college. I didn't have the best reputation, which had more to do with some of the girls I hung out with than me. Whenever I dated a guy seriously, which definitely wasn't often, they would be "warned" by others about who they felt I was.

Jose of course had heard these things about me, and although I had changed my life completely for the better and let go of my past, there was still hesitation because men want to marry the good girl, and I had definitely not been that. Couple this with the fact that I had a daughter and had also had abortions; well this would make any guy head for the hills. Jose had been wild, too, but guys aren't scrutinized as we are.

We were married three years ago, June 06, 2010. I would say our story is different than most because we didn't actually date. In fact, we were the furthest thing from a couple. I knew him because he'd dated my best friend our freshman year of college, and years later I was his roommate's girlfriend. In that time, he had tried dating four more of my friends, so he was not looking at me for marriage.

One day, seemingly out of the blue, he made a change and decided that he was going to live for God, go to church—all that.

I saw this change, and we instantly became close. His roommate and I had broken up, and we started going to the same church. We spent a lot of time together, and the change that I saw made him appealing to me, but I never said anything to him about it. In my eyes, he was perfect, physically and spiritually.

I just made sure I was very visible. We talked every day and hung out every night after I got off work. We shared personal stories and grew very close in a short amount of time, but like I said, we never dated—at least in the way most people think. We weren't necessarily a couple, just friends that spent time together, went out to eat occasionally, and hung out at church.

When he learned some of the less savory facts about me, he was put off.

His old friends tried to put ideas in his head negatively about me as well.

Because of our shared new views on life and marriage, we grew closer, but never became intimate with one another, which was a struggle, but helped him see that I was a reformed bad girl. His mind was put to ease about who I had been and the person I had become, the more he saw me in the church and the more he saw me pull away from my old life.

Gradually, he came to see that, like him, I had let go of everything and everybody that had been a weight and bad influence in my life, but unlike with him, it was harder to get people to believe I had changed paths and was now on the high road. He had easily done the same, and that shared change in paths was finally enough to get our paths to collide—coupled with the ministers in our church saying we should be together.

Other women had their eye on him because he is a good-looking, God-fearing man, which is something all the single women in the church desire. The only advantage I had was that I became a friend first. Although we had already known each other, we hadn't really conversed or spent much time together doing anything productive. I hear a lot of people say they married their best friend, and that's basically what we had become. We had let go of so many (toxic) people in our lives that we didn't have much more than each other.

I really wanted him to like me, so I did the things he liked to do. I didn't go outside of who I was, but I did do things with him that he enjoyed. We worked out together, we ate together, and I asked his advice on things, sometimes just to have something to talk with him about. I also made sure that whenever I was going to see him, I was dressed nicely. I was mostly a T-shirt and jeans kind of girl outside of work, but for him I put more effort into my looks. The church that we were going to wasn't my first choice, but because he was there and we were getting closer, I continued to go there regularly and was even baptized there.

I also have to say, we both love to cook, which I found out about him while dating his roommate. Even when I was with his roommate, I always wanted him to enjoy my cooking. When we became friends, I would constantly cook food for him. Sometimes, I would cook dinner and take it to his house, and other times I would cook something and bring it to him at work for lunch. I am also a woman that likes to buy things for her man, and even though he isn't a man who likes gifts, I still got things for him. When he started a new job, I bought his work shoes and belts and helped him get the rest of his work wardrobe as well.

One Wednesday night after church service, we were sitting around listening to music with a friend at his apartment. It just sort of felt like there was something different in the air that night; maybe I already knew subconsciously. After our friend left, it was just the two of us.

In my mind, I was thinking as we talked, "I hope he asks me to marry him."

He began telling me how he felt about me, "Raya, you make me happy. I'm happier when I'm with you than anyone else or doing anything else."

I got really nervous.

As he finished, he said, "I feel like I could spend the rest of his life with you."

I jumped up and said, "Let's get married!"

He agreed.

So, I guess I sort of proposed. Maybe I didn't let him finish, but that's how it happened. We lived together five days before we got married.

That's how I got him to marry me. I just stayed on his radar and made sure that he had a good impression of me and showed him what life would be like with me as his wife; how I would take care of him just as I felt he would take care of me. Three years later and coming up on our fourth anniversary, we're still together, and the main reason is our faith, which is what brought us together in the first place.

#28 ANGELA AND STUART

In 1997, I met a man at work. I was only 15 years old and working in a tobacco field. My best friend's father had gotten me and her jobs cropping tobacco for the summer. This was a very dirty job, and there was no way for either of us to look appealing to any man with tobacco juice and muddy clothes on us. My best friend and I drove up to the field on our first day of work. I was in high school, and I was popular with the boys. I was one of those girls that made it a point to put on flashy clothes and lots of makeup before I left for school. I was very worried about my image.

Well, we stepped out of her car and walked over to the harvester where we would be working. The man that hired us walked up and introduced himself to us. Neither of us had worked in tobacco before, so he found someone to come work alongside us and instruct us in the right ways to hand tobacco and crop tobacco.

The job was easy enough, but we were tired at the end of the day. We worked Monday through Friday and usually were paid on Friday afternoon. After we got our first paychecks, we headed down to the shopping mall to buy some things.

The second week of work was different for me. The man that I was working for had a son. This son had been away at college for the first week, so we hadn't met him yet. I was amazed when this old car pulled up and this dark haired man with the most beautiful blue eyes emerged. His clothes were stained, and his hat covered most of his face. He even seemed a little shy, looking down while we walked by. Being the crazy kid I was, I walked over to him and introduced myself.

"Hello, I'm Angela… and you are?"

"Uh, hi. I'm Stuart."

After this brief introduction, he and I became inseparable. I fell in love immediately. The only issue was he was in college, and I was still in high school.

It came time for him to go back to college. I was sad, and so was he. He found himself driving every weekend, back home to see me. Our evenings were spent on the phone together. We never imagined how much we would miss each other during the week.

One evening, I started talking about ways we could be together every day. I asked him about marriage. He said he would love to be married, but his parents were very strict about him finishing college prior to getting married. They were afraid of their son quitting school or starting a family before graduation.

After that conversation, I felt as if we would never be married, or at best, we would have to wait two years until he completed his college education. I felt as if I needed to make a decision. Could I go on missing him this much but also knowing that I had another couple of years to wait? Would he ever ask me to marry him? He was the type that listened to his parents and did as they asked.

The next December came, and Stuart told me he had a surprise for me. His parents were out of town, and he was cooking dinner for me. At 7 pm, he arrived at my house to pick me up for our date. I dressed nice and practically ran out the door to meet him. Our kisses were very loving. He walked around and opened up the car door for me. We drove to his parent's house. We arrived, and he unlocked the door. On the kitchen table were flowers and a beautiful table setting. There was food cooking on the stove with a beautiful fire in the fireplace and candles burning around the room. This was very romantic.

I thought, "This night is the night! He's going to ask me to marry him!"

Dinner and the conversation were nice. I could not help myself but believe that any minute he would get down on one knee and pop the question.

On the corner of the table, I saw a box. The box was very small and shaped like a diamond ring box. I was so excited!

After dinner, we went to the living room. I could not help but notice that the small box was missing. He and I sat and talked for hours, and no box or getting down on one knee happened.

Right before he was going to drive me home, he said, "Angie, I have something for you."

My heart hit the floor when he handed me the small box. I just knew he was asking me to marry him tonight. I skittishly opened the box. My heart sank. Inside the box was the most beautiful birthstone ring I had ever seen. I had to act like it was great because it really was a beautiful ring, but inside I was just sad and disappointed that he had not proposed.

On one of our later conversations, he again took the time to explain that he needed to complete college before marriage.

I told him, "If we marry, we could help each other."

Living together was never an option.

He began coming home less and less, but we still dated, and we still talked on the phone. He was away at college again, and I was again in high school. The summer had been the same, with us working together in his dad's tobacco patch. Yes, we had a great summer. Two kids in love. Now, reality was setting in.

I asked him point blank one night, "Stuart, do you think we will ever get married?"

"Maybe."

Well girls, "Maybe" was not what I wanted to hear. Over the next year, I tried to cut my ties with him. I let him call me; I never called him anymore. I realized I wasn't even officially his girlfriend. I went on a few first dates with other guys, but never dated the same guy twice. I was still hoping, but giving up fast.

The year proceeded until he came home for Christmas holidays again. He called and asked me out to breakfast, and I agreed to go.

He drove over to my house to pick me up. Before breakfast, he and I went down to the river. We walked on the bridge, and he stopped me. He turned me around and gave me a kiss. He got on one knee and finally proposed for me to marry him. I got my ring, and I got my proposal. He finally agreed to get married, and I was beside myself. I was happy, and we lived happily ever after. It never pays to underestimate the power of love and God's plans for us all. We were married in 1999.

#29 LEAH AND ERIK

On May 18th of 2004, I knew I would spend the rest of my life with him. This fateful day was the day of our high school prom. Yes. Braces, puffy lace, and Britney Spears blasting in the background. This was the ultimate beginning to a high school fairy tale. Erik had been the funny guy in my class for almost two years, and ever since the first day when he came into the classroom loudly and dramatically singing the chorus of Hilary Duff's "So Yesterday," I was hooked on him. Since then, he and I had always been pretty good friends, but of course, I had always wanted us to be more than that.

Prom was approaching.

We were only sophomores, but I was growing more and more anxious. Every time Erik and I would talk, I would hope to God that he would ask me to be his date. The day before the prom, I had given up hope on going. I figured I'd stay home and study for that awful algebra test I knew was coming, and maybe watch a little bit of Fresh Prince before bed. The day was winding up at school, and Erik came running up to me, panting and gasping.

I giggled, "Why the rush?"

"Did you know prom is tomorrow?" He was still panting.

I smiled innocently. "Wow, I guess it is. I really haven't thought..."

He cut me off. "Well, are you going with

somebody?"

"No, I'm not."

He ran his fingers through his curly hair. "Well...Uh. Do you think...Maybe we could go together?"

I looked at the ground and grinned. "Well yeah, that would be cool."

His eyes lit up, and he slung his backpack over his shoulder. "Alright, cool! I'll pick you up at 6!"

We really hit it off that night, and it was the first time I was ever kissed. He told me that he had always liked me, and that he never had the guts to ask me if I felt the same way. That night was our first date. And little did we know, there would be three years worth of dates to follow. We were thoroughly attached to each other, and head-over-heels in love.

After high school, we both got busy starting our lives. Erik started working full time at a local car shop, and I worked as a part-time secretary for a local law firm while going to community college at the same time. We were both very busy people, but always managed to make time to spend together.

I was living with my parents at the time, and he had gotten an apartment in town. After a few months of living there by himself, he was getting lonely.

He said, "Maybe we should move in together, so we don't have to spend so much time away from each other?"

As much as I loved the idea of spending every day and night with him, something didn't feel right about the situation. I told him, "I'll think about it and get back to you when I reach a conclusion."

About a week after he asked me, I went to work

and school and then decided to stop by his place on my way home to discuss this issue that had been rolling around in my head all day.

I knocked on the door, and about a minute later he answered it, smiling and happy as always. We sat down on his couch.

"Erik, I really love you and I do want to be with you always."

He started to hug me, but I held up my hand to show I wasn't finished.

"I've decided after much thought and much prayer that I can't bring myself to move in with you. I was raised in a Christian family with morals that go against living together before marriage, and I won't violate those guidelines."

He thoughtfully looked at me and said, "You know, I never looked at it that way. I don't want you to move in if it goes against your beliefs and makes you uncomfortable. That's the very last thing I'd ever want."

Relieved that he understood, I forgot about the issue, and we went back to our usual lives. All was well with our relationship, but a little part of me was let down. I was a bit sad that we couldn't spend all of our time together, and a few months later, I was starting to rethink my concerns on moving in with him. I never voiced this sadness with Erik, so he thought all was fine with me. He seemed so happy and excited every time he saw me, and it always made me forget the sadness that I felt about the subject, so I kept my feelings to myself.

A couple months later, On August 8th of 2008 (my birthday), Erik and I went to the summer festival that our town has by the beach every year. We went out to dinner and then walked around the festival for a couple hours. He seemed to be acting really strange that day. He was nervous and didn't hardly eat anything the whole day.

I was getting anxious, and of course was thinking the worst: "What's going on? Why is he acting strange? Is he going to break up with me?

As the sun was starting to go down, we decided to go to the pier and watch the sunset. We sat down next to each other, and I wrapped my arms around him. He still seemed restless and anxious, just as he'd been all day. He untangled himself from me and looked in my eyes. He seemed to relax and ran his fingers through my hair.

"Leah, I've been thinking..." He began shakily, "You and I have been together for a long time... And I've been thinking for the past couple months."

He got down in front on me on one knee and grabbed both my hands. He looked into my eyes for a moment, and then reached in his pocket. He pulled out a little pink box and slowly opened it.

I couldn't breathe.

Tears were streaming down my face.

He looked at me and said, "Leah...You are the woman that I love with all my heart, and I would love nothing better than to spend the rest of my nights and days with the woman of my dreams. Will you marry me?"

In shock, and through my tears of joy, I gladly accepted. And on July 20, 2009, we started our happily ever after.

#30 CARLA AND MANNIE

We got married on October 9, 1993. Thinking back, it's so incredibly hard to believe it will be twenty years of marriage this year. It wasn't an easy path to get there... or here. And twenty years? Aren't people who have been married for twenty years old? I used to think so. My kids may think so. But here we are twenty years later, still going strong. And to think, it took some convincing to get where we are today.

We met in January of 1990 at a bar. We had both come off long, involved relationships. Mine was a 2 year high school romance, and his was a four year serious relationship. They almost got engaged. So, when we met, neither of us was really looking for a commitment. We got along well, had much in common, and decided that we would become friends.

As our friendship developed over the summer of 1990, we realized that we were falling in love, and even though we were both scared to take the next step in becoming exclusive, we did. However, it did not come easy, and we did end up splitting apart a few times, but we were always drawn back to each other.

You know how they say, "If you love someone, let them go, and if it was meant to be, you'll find your way back"? Well, that always happened to us. We would split up, and two weeks later find ourselves on another date. Your heart has a way of controlling your mind when you're in love.

After our last break-up a few weeks before Christmas 1990, we decided to give it just one more try. We promised that if we decided to break-up one more time, that was it; we would never get back together. Well, it worked, because 22 years later we're still back together.

Fast forward to 1992. Two years into our relationship, both of us approaching our late twenties, we had that discussion: marriage. But, there again was that commitment issue. He had already been close to engagement, and that was when they broke up, so he was really, really nervous to get to that next point. We shopped around for rings, nothing serious, but he was still very hesitant. We remembered our promise to each other, but he was really scared to take the plunge.

So, I had some convincing to do.

His parents had recently divorced, so his fear of commitment was really hitting a new high. After more than twenty years of marriage and four kids, his father found someone else. I think it hit my husband the hardest, as the oldest kid. They waited until their youngest graduated high school and then split. To this day, my husband does not have a good relationship with his father. I can count on my fingers the number of times my father-in-law has seen my kids (and our oldest is 16).

He felt torn: can you devote that much time to someone and still end it after so much investment? What if he found someone else? Did he want to subject me to that kind of pain?

I told him, "Well, what if I found someone else? We can't predict the future, but we can work our butts off to make sure those fears don't become a reality. And besides, my parents have been together for almost 40 years. Not everyone gets a divorce."

We just had to roll the dice and take the gamble. We wanted to be together. We loved each other enough. We both wanted a family; that was something we never questioned. Did we want to wait until we were older to start that family? In thinking back, I didn't have my kids until age 29 and 34 because of difficulties getting pregnant. Imagine if we had waited. I might not have had any children. And I can't even imagine a day without my kids.

His next argument was money. Financially, we could have been in a better position.

But my argument there: are we ever going to be in a position where we will be 100% set for life, financially?

He agreed: probably not.

If you wait until you're financially able to marry and start a family, you're going to be waiting your entire life. Understandably, you want to be sure to have a good job and a bright outlook on your career, but if you're waiting to have $50,000 in the bank, or your future child's college fund paid for, think again.

We only get one chance. One try. This is the only time that God has given us on Earth, and it goes by incredibly fast. I think sometimes we forget this is our only shot. We took risks; we took gambles; we followed our hearts. Twenty years later, we're not looking back and saying "what if?"

No regrets.

We can't approach every decision we make in life with that outlook, but for marriage, for long-term "let's-grow-old-together-his-and-her-towels"?

Follow your heart.

Yes, some marriages fail. But many don't. Love is something to be treasured, a gift. If God brought you two together, why defy that? But, be sure you're both in 100%. There's got to be that certainty that you both have this commitment in your heart. The fear will go away. My husband's did, and twenty years and two kids later, there's no doubt the decision to get married was the right one.

#31 MICHELLE AND GEORGE

From the time we started dating to the day we were married was exactly six months. My husband and I have been married since 2002, and I must say our courtship was quite the whirlwind.

I attribute our short engagement to two factors:
1) I had twin 1-year-old boys.
2) I didn't sleep with him until we were married.

I know that may seem old fashioned, but it worked twice for me.

My first husband and I dated for exactly 7 months before we were married because I would not sleep with him, either. I did not want to live together, since I felt that would surely lead to a stagnant relationship that would not move forward. I had seen this with so many of my girlfriends, I felt I needed to break this cycle. This one simple tactic has worked for me twice. My first husband and I were married for 5 years. We had twins in March of 2000, and in June of that same year he tragically passed away in his sleep, leaving me a widow with 3-month-old twins.

I had to completely rebuild my life, and it was a year later that I met my current husband. I felt like it would be even more difficult to get married this time, since I not only had one baby, but two!

I think at first he was a bit overwhelmed, so we just focused on being great friends. I think marrying your best guy friend is one of the best choices you can make. After we became really close friends, one day he told me that he didn't want to imagine his life without me in it (and the boys, too). It was then that we started to be romantically involved. It was difficult to not cross that physical barrier, but I am so glad that I didn't because I can tell my daughter (we had her after 3 years of marriage) that it is possible to save yourself for marriage.

Staying celibate during our dating also helped my husband see that he wanted to be married; it was actually his idea first. I felt he wasn't entirely ready to raise children, but he was able to convince me otherwise. His only objection was that he felt I should have dated more men before settling down with him! By not having a physical aspect to our dating, it made us learn how to communicate and to value what each of us was thinking, rather than to base our relationship on passion, which we all know usually only lasts for 6-7 months. I can honestly say our passion lasted for 3 years until we had our daughter, at which time our focus shifted.

I also love being able to tell the story to my children. The boys will soon be teenagers. I feel that they see our union as special and worthy of respect because we showed restraint. I wish my first husband was still around to see his amazing sons, but I am so grateful that they have the father they have now.

#32 CLARE AND JOEY

I always thought I would be proposed to in some grandiose way that I would be able to tell my grand kids about, but that's not how it happened with me and Joey. We would have long drawn out arguments about getting married and why I wanted to, and he just couldn't understand the importance of it. I specifically remember one night we were discussing our difference of opinion.

He kept telling me:

"It's pointless to get married."

Of course, I didn't take kindly to it and promptly told him:

"It means we love each other and want to spend the rest of our lives together."

You know the answer I got:

"Of course we love each other. We live together, and I do want to spend my life with you, but we don't need to get married to do that."

You know how it is when you talk to certain types of people and they see the world in black and white? Well, this is my husband to a T. No matter how much I complained about wanting to be married for love or for our families or even to show the world that we were together, he would always have something to say that just made sense, and that I really couldn't argue with, such as:

"Do you really care what anyone else thinks?"

Over and over he would say it, with that prissy holier-than-thou attitude.

I knew then just like I know now that I truly love my husband, but he just doesn't open his eyes to see how he affects the ones around him.

Now, my mom was really sick when I was growing up, and we all knew that she wasn't going to live much longer, so that was the card I finally had to pull out of my bag in order to get him to at least agree with me. So during one of our famous conversations that can go on for days and be picked back up at any time without missing a beat, I snuck that one in.

I know; I know. It's a low blow to use your dying mother, but I really did want her to see us get married, and I wasn't getting any younger, either.

Joey told me, "Fine, but don't you care that I don't think we're ready for this? It doesn't really make me happy to be rushed."

Rushed! We'd been living together for two years! I was so done with that. You can bet what my reply was.

"Well, if you want to stay with me, then you'll get over it."

As fast as I could get him in the car, we were off to the jewelers to buy the engagement ring. I already knew I wanted a plain solitaire diamond, so it wasn't any big deal to find what I liked. That weekend, we announced our engagement to our parents.

And, it really did make my mom so happy. It's one thing to this day that I remember clearly making her smile when she was surrounded by pain, and I will never regret rushing my husband along. I actually had to wait for my mom to get out of the hospital in order to go dress shopping, but she was there and helped me pick out a dress.

We were planning the wedding for the following summer and were looking at different venues and options when I got the call that my mom had died. She never did get to see me on my wedding day, but at least she got to see me in my wedding dress.

Of course, I had to give Joey the option of moving back the wedding or canceling it altogether, since I had told him I really wanted my mom to see it and be happy. Thankfully, he did the right thing and told me to keep on planning it, if that was what made me happy. So I did.

Finally, summer was rolling around and we were all set to be married the following month in July of 2004. Like any bride, I couldn't wait and was frantic getting everything done, when catastrophe hit us again.

Joey's little brother David, who I graduated from high school with, came in to town to be fitted for his tux. He was to be our best man. Since he was only in town for the weekend, we wanted to all spend as much time together as we could, so we took our motorcycles to the local drag racing track. Our entire families watched him crash and die on the track that night, one month before our wedding. Nothing could take away the pain of that moment.

I told Joey and his parents, "We have to cancel the wedding. It's just too soon. It's not right to have it so soon."

Once again, Joey stepped up.

"We're having the wedding. It may not be the way each of you envisioned, but it would make Clare's mother and David happy. Most of all, I want to be married to Clare, and that's what matters."

A month later, we were married. No one stood in the best man's spot because David was still there in our hearts. Candles were lit on the altar, one for my mom and one for my brother-in-law. I wore the dress my mother picked out, and we both realized it wasn't about making everyone else happy, just ourselves.

#33 ELIZABETH AND MIKE

When I met Mike in 2008, he was not ready to settle down, but he was the sweetest man I had ever met, so I decided to see where it would go. When I brought up marriage, he froze instantly. We dated for several months before I asked him why he was so against marriage. His biggest fear was that he would invest so much time and effort to have the marriage end in divorce. He had been burned in previous relationships and was afraid it would happen again. The other problem he had with marriage was being tied down and the fear that we wouldn't always be in love like we were then.

One night, he came over and said he had a very important question to ask me.

I thought, "Finally, he is going to propose!"

He sat down next to me and said "Elizabeth, will you..."

"Oh! Here we go!" I thought.

"...move in with me?"

I freaked out and was like, "What?"

He said, "I'm ready to take the next step, but still not ready for marriage."

I was so mad I wanted to scream but knew it wouldn't do any good.

I told him, "We can move in together, but you are going to marry me eventually."

His only response was "We'll see."

I then told him, "You have six months to propose, and we will not be having sex until you do!"

We had been living together for a couple of months when my parents invited us on a family vacation to Florida for New Year's. This was a perfect way to bring up the whole marriage issue again. I mentioned how perfect a beach proposal at midnight on New Year's would be. He seemed to shrug it off.

I told myself, "If he's not willing to marry me, then it's probably time to move on."

One day, we were looking up airfare for our trip, and he went to take a shower. While he was in the shower, I started looking at engagement rings. I may have "accidentally" left one of the engagement ring photos open on the computer for him to see.

After he got dressed, he came over to the computer and was like "That doesn't look like airfare."

I just smiled and said, "I think its time to take the next step. Don't you like this ring?"

I swear, it was like a deer in headlights. His eyes got all big, and he didn't say a word.

I just laughed, said, "Think about it," and walked away.

While I was packing for our trip, I came across a box from a jewelry store and got all excited. He hadn't mentioned ever going to even look at a jewelry store, and I couldn't imagine what would have changed his mind. I figured it was probably a necklace or something, not a ring. I didn't look, and nor did I mention the box the whole time we packed. Before we left, I checked the drawer and there was no box, so I assumed he had packed it.

Again, I said not a word about finding the box because I was afraid of what the answer might have been.

We arrived in Florida and were on the beach shortly before midnight. I was so excited. There were bonfires, fireworks, and champagne! But, no proposal. The next night, he took me to a nice restaurant, just the two of us. The food was amazing! But, no proposal. I will admit I was a little preoccupied by the whole marriage thing. I loved him, but I couldn't see myself starting a family with someone who wouldn't marry me.

On the last night of our trip, we were walking down the beach collecting shells to take home. He was right beside me, and suddenly I looked over and he was gone. I turned around and saw him on his knees, intently staring at the sand.

I ran back and said, "What are you looking at?"

He said, "I thought I saw something sparkle in the sand."

I looked down, and sure enough, there was the most gorgeous ring in the sand.

"Wow! Someone is sure going to miss that!"

He smiled and said, "Yea, you if you don't pick it up!"

I was surprised that he would say that since I truly thought someone had lost it. I picked up the ring and looked at him as he got on one knee.

"Elizabeth, will you marry me?"

I was speechless and smiling like an idiot when I finally said:

"Well, its about time. Of course I will!"

On the flight home, all I could think about was picking a dress, setting a date, and sending out invitations. Of course, Mister Take-it-slow was not ready to do any of that. He couldn't see why we needed to rush to get married and wanted to have a long engagement. I, on the other had, was like a kid on Christmas. I wanted to see and do it all. We finally began discussing wedding plans the following January. He wanted a summer wedding so we could have it outdoors. I wasn't picky on when so long as it was within the year.

We finally decided on a small church wedding. We were married on June 6, 2010 in a small church surrounded by our family and best friends. We had a small reception at a local café. The best words I had ever heard were, "I now pronounce you man and wife." We have been married for two and a half years and have 2 beautiful daughters. We have had our ups and downs but always come out on top, and we are still in love.

#34 DAN AND AMANDA ROBBINS

We decided to live together five years ago because we wanted to combine our finances. We were both struggling to pay our mortgages, so we sold those two and bought a house together. In many ways, he was already like my husband at that point, but we didn't have the official titles of husband and wife. He never wanted to marry me, but I made him marry me. I didn't want to just live with him anymore. I wanted to be able to call him my husband, not just my boyfriend.

His main reason for objecting to marry me was the divorce rate is so high, and he didn't want to be a statistic. He thought what we had was good enough, and he didn't want to ruin what we had going. He had several friends who went through the process of divorce, but the divorce that really affected him was that of his own parents. It was very damaging to him that his parents openly fought their custody battle in front of him, and he blamed himself for it. This is also the reason he had reservations about having any kids of our own.

With counseling, he was able to realize it wasn't his fault his parents got a divorce, but he still had negative views about becoming a husband. He said he had all he needed with me as his girlfriend.

The next word battle we had was the battle for kids.

"Amanda, my childhood was a mess. My parents were always yelling at each other through the walls of our apartment and slamming doors and crying. It was an awful disaster. I promised myself I would never ever inflict that on anyone, so I am never having kids."

"We have a different situation than your parents though, Dan. They decided on their own account to make the divorce an ugly one. We are in a happy relationship, so hopefully there will be no need for divorce. However, if there is a need for a divorce, we can choose to make the divorce as civil as possible."

It took many many conversations like that one, but he finally agreed to have kids with me because he came to realize that what I was saying was right. The kids will be born into a loving relationship, and the relationship will always be a loving one for the kids' sake. I could see that he was still nervous, but at least he agreed to have kids with me. So then I played my hand.

I asked, "Wouldn't our kids be better off if their parents were married?"

He just looked at me.

I knew to be quiet for a while.

I also wanted to get his work's health insurance because I didn't have any. I made too much money to get the state insurance, and my job didn't offer any health insurance. Since he cares about my health, he also agreed that I needed to get health insurance through his work.

Not only did I want him as my husband because I loved him, I pointed out there were a lot of practical reasons to get married. He agreed that it would make our financial situation better, so he agreed to marry me.

I didn't mind being long-term boyfriend and girlfriend, but I wanted to advance myself to the next level.

I didn't believe in having children until I was married, so I also wanted to get married to have kids. I knew I'd have to convince my boyfriend that we can do this differently than his parents. The custody situation is as civil or as bad as you make it.

We got married last week, and it was a beautiful ceremony. Since my husband's parents refuse to be in the same room together, only his mother came. My mother lost her battle with breast cancer a couple years ago, so only my dad could come to the wedding. In addition, we had about 100 guests of friends and family members. We had the ceremony on the beach, and the reception was at a hall. Since I come from a big family, I had my four siblings at the wedding and their immediate families there. I decided to let their kids come.

#35 LINDA AND DAN

They called us high-school sweethearts, and I guess that was exactly what we were, and still are. We met at our small town of Jackson Ohio's yearly Apple Festival, where I winked at him, actually just to make my cousin, who I was with at the Festival, laugh at me for doing something so bold, since I was usually a shy person.

Dan eventually had a friend of mine ask me, "Would you ever go out with Dan?"

I shockingly said, "Yes."

From then on, we were hardly ever apart. I was madly in love with him, and he with me. We stayed together through high school.

Even though we were fresh out of high school and still very young, at graduation I thought:

"Now we can finally get married."

To my surprise and disappointment, he never asked. He just acted like things were OK the way they were, but they were not, for me at least.

I didn't understand why he didn't want to get married, and then I met his mother.

She'd been divorced by the time he was two years old and had never married again. She had been hurt so bad that she hated marriage, and for her whole life, she talked against it to everyone she ever met. I then realized this was the reason he didn't want to get married, why he felt getting married just made people's relationships worse.

I felt totally helpless, and I even felt like maybe we didn't belong together after all, even though I loved him immensely. So I decided that I would talk to my cousin Angie, who was like a sister to me.

She said, "Why don't you give him an ultimatum? Tell him either he marries you, or you and him are over for good."

I thought about what she said and decided I would do just that, once I got the nerve.

I finally got the nerve to tell him, "I love you, but if you can't marry me, then what's the sense in being together in a relationship that's going nowhere?"

He just looked down as I was telling him this, like I had just broken his heart, and he never said a word, just sat there.

I said "Are you going to say something to me?"

But he just sat there.

So, I got up with an angry look on my face and left him sitting there.

For about a month, we never talked and never saw each other. And then finally one day I saw him at a restaurant with his friends.

He smiled at me and said "Can I talk to you?"

"Yes."

And finally, there and then, he poured out his heart to me.

"I truly love you, and I couldn't live without you. I do want to marry you, but I'm afraid to ask because I already messed up, and I don't think you'll give me a second chance."

We finally got married July 11, 1992 at Hammertown Lake, under a grove of oak trees. It was a small wedding with a few family and friends. Me and my husband Dan have been married now going on twenty-one years, and we are still madly in love, and have four children.

Ladies, I believe you should always be up front on what you want out of a relationship, especially if its a serious one. If he truly loves you, then he will understand and recognize when something is especially important to you, even if its a marriage proposal. It may hurt sometimes to express your wants and needs to someone special, but it can lead to something very fulfilling and wonderful.

#36 JEN AND MIKE

I met him on a blind date. I was a week shy of 20, and he was a frat boy in his senior year. I first saw him the day we were set up, and instantly I knew this was my last first date. We got along great! I kept waiting to find something wrong with him, but nothing ever was wrong.

For my part, one of my big problems in previous relationships had been remaking myself to be what the guy wanted, so while I was open-minded with Mike, I did not just do what he wanted because he wanted to. I think one of the reasons we worked was that I was determined to be myself with him.

I told myself, "This will work, or it won't, but I'm not going to pretend to be something I'm not."

That summer full of pizza, beer, and living on credit came and went. In the fall, we moved in together at a mutual friend's house, but we never talked about marriage. I was 20, he was 22, and I was scared to even bring marriage up because I didn't want to rock the boat. I took each day as it came, and we made plans for no further in the future than the weekend.

The first sign that made me think we might get married was him accepting a dirty, stinky, but decently paid job locally and turning down a more glamorous one down south, 10 hours away from me. I had the typical new grad job of summer nanny, so while I was putting on sunblock to go to work, he was donning a hard hat to go to his first engineering job, in a factory in Brooklyn.

Those two years in what we called "frat house, part 2" were a time of bonding. We shared a house with 5 others. I started playing the video games he loved and found out that I liked them, too. I was the cool girlfriend because I played games with him. I kept an open mind, and if I didn't have anything against an idea I would try it, and usually it was fun. We had fun together, and at the time, that was enough. We were still only 22 and 24, starting our first 'grown up' jobs.

Soon, Mike got a fabulous offer for a job in Wisconsin—a thousand miles from home for me.

When the offer was on the table, he looked at me and said:

"Will you come with me? I won't go without you."

I thought to myself, "How deep will I go before I get married?"

I didn't want to lose him, though, and besides, Wisconsin sounded like an adventure, right?

So, I smiled and said, "Yes," hoping that someday soon I would be saying yes to a much more important question.

We fit 100% of our life in a small rented U-haul truck and set out for adventure. The apartment we shared in Wisconsin was our little nest, our first time totally interdependent. So far from home and friends, we grew closer.

At 23 and 25, the question of marriage was not so remote anymore.

I started to bring it up, and the more I talked about it, the more irritated he got. He thought we were too young to get married. He thought we were just not ready;

we had no savings, and we were under a mountain of debt.

I was afraid. I was far from home, intertwined with this guy I had grown to love and depend on, but he seemed way too content to keep the status quo. I decided to just drop it and give it time. A year from now, we would be older, more mature, and perhaps ready. My plan was to keep having fun, keep being true to myself, keep being loving—and most important in my mind, not turn into a crazy girl fixated on marriage.

And then, the annoying question started, from friends, co-workers, acquaintances, family, and even strangers:

"So, when are you two getting married?"

As if I knew!

I kept my cool and laughed it off. Maybe I'm old fashioned, but I wanted him to ask. I wanted him to want to ask.

We bought a car together and made plans for the future. Together, we figured out a plan to get ourselves out of debt: his salary covered all our expenses and loan payments, so the temp job I got went 100% to pay off old debt. Every month, a different credit card got a fat check. It felt good to get out of debt; it felt great to start saving.

When we started to talk "house," I started to get serious about the marriage thing. I didn't want to own real estate together without being married. That was my line in the sand. But, we were still a long way from a down payment, so it was not like I was holding a gun to his head.

One day in March, Mike had a big smile after a conversation with his sister, who did our taxes.

I asked, "So, how much is our refund?"

He said with a grin "Nan filed us jointly since we meet the criteria, so we are getting 7 thousand back!"

I looked at him and said, "Jointly?"

And that was the last word I said for the next 12 hours. The only way I would answer him was to moo like a cow. I think he got the memo.

We were out of debt except for car loans. We were 24 and 26, and we had been together 5 years. I didn't know what else to do, but life rolled on, and we were busy with life.

That May, he asked me to meet him for lunch.

I thought nothing of it, then all of a sudden he was on one knee, proposing. It took my brain a minute to catch up to what my ears were hearing. I actually missed the beginning of what he said, but the last line was:

"And Jen, will you promise to never moo again?"

I'm sure that sounded crazy to everyone else in the restaurant, but I knew exactly what he meant.

We have been married since November 6, 2004, a month before my 25th birthday. I asked him what finally convinced him, and he said we had gotten out of debt, we had decent jobs, we were old enough to know what we wanted for sure, and he loved me (not in that order). He wanted to get a house, and I had made it clear I wanted to get married first. I think that mooing must have played into it, but more importantly, I think being happy no matter what did it.

#37 VALERIE AND CRAIG

Craig and I both worked third shift at a local grocery store. He was working stock, and I was a cashier. We talked on occasion, and one day he walked up and gave me his number and told me to call if I just wanted to hang out or whatever. So, about three days later I decided to call him, and we talked for about 2 hours. We went out later that week for coffee, and after talking for a little while I learned he had four children from a previous marriage, and I told him I also had four children from a previous marriage. We decided even though there were eight children between us, we would try our hand at fate. Then, in December we found out that we were expecting another child.

We couldn't have been happier, except the idea of being married appealed to me and scared him to death. We talked all the time about marriage. I was willing to marry him because I knew we were meant for one another. After that first bad experience he had, he was really skeptical of getting married again.

So, I tried to convince him with talk and told him I would do whatever it took for him to understand I wasn't that way. It didn't work, and I thought I had truly lost the battle and that I was going to be with this man forever with no ring or name to go with it.

So, I tried getting his mother on my side. I had her talk to him, and she told him she thought it was a great idea and that she really liked me. The only reason why I went there was because he is very close with his mother.

Unfortunately, that didn't work, either. He told her he just didn't know if he could do it again.

Then, everything that I had been working for on the marriage aspect got put on hold.

We found out our unborn son had a cyst on his kidney, and they thought it might be cancerous. I was put on immediate bed rest, and we spent the next couple of months running to and from ultrasounds and doctor appointments to make sure our little man was doing OK. My water broke when guests were about to arrive for my oldest child's 10th birthday party, and I was in hard labor.

So, I tried to use our son's birth as a reason to get married.

I told Craig, "Our son is such a miracle, and I always want to be with you, so why don't we get married?"

He finally said, "Maybe."

It was a lot closer than a no.

So, over the next few weeks I talked with his mother and my sister about what I could do or say to convince him to tie the knot. I did everything I could think of. We went out for nice romantic dinners and came home to a fireplace and candlelight, and I tried to talk to him about it then, but that didn't work. I talked with one of his buddies and thought if he could convince him, then I was willing to give it a try.

So, Craig and his buddy went hunting for the day, and when he came home I did my normal asking him how his day was. He told me his buddy had mentioned he should marry me, that he really liked me. Then, he told me they had discussed it for a while, but he told his buddy that it wasn't going to happen. He just couldn't do it. At this point, I couldn't help but think that we were never going to tie the knot, no matter what I tried.

I was at his mom's one afternoon while he was working.

She told me, "He has always loved it in North Carolina, where he was born and raised."

At that moment, it was like a light bulb had just turned on in my head.

So, we discussed a vacation to North Carolina and decided it was a much needed break for us both. We decided we wanted to go to Myrtle Beach, South Carolina instead, but we were going to make stops in North Carolina along the way. A month later, we were on the road to our vacation destination. We had only made one stop in North Carolina and that was at Mulberry. Then we finally made it to our vacation condo on the front row of the beach with a nice balcony overlooking the ocean.

This was a place that you would dream about taking a honeymoon at. Can you understand where I was going with this last attempt to convince him to tie the knot? We went sightseeing and spent wonderful evenings on the beach just talking about everything. About 3 days into our trip, we had stopped by a little shop just over the border in North Carolina. This place had everything, including a Christmas shop. We just happened to walk into a jewelry store, and there was the most beautiful set of rings I had ever seen. I showed them to him, and we even tried them on. We however did not purchase them.

The next morning when I woke up, he was not at the condo. He left a note saying he'd run up to grab some breakfast and would be right back. We spent the whole day on the beach, and when night fell he went to the condo and grabbed a radio we had taken with us and we danced on the beach just as the moon was reaching its high.

Then, he dropped to one knee and proposed with the same ring we had looked at the day before.

Of course I said yes, and I couldn't be happier my plan had worked.

When we got home, I had fun showing everyone the ring. I was so happy that I convinced him. A week after we got back home, we had a little church wedding, and I was finally a Mrs. I may have had to push the issue, but I couldn't be happier. It was the best decision and most worthwhile fight I have ever had in my life!

#38 LEAH MAC

I met my husband back in 2009, by chance. I had gone out to dinner with friends, and they decided to leave early to get home to their own houses and husbands. I, however, had been divorced for quite a bit of time and thus only had my daughter to care for. She was spending the weekend with my sister, and I just really did not want to go home to an empty house yet again.

I decided to make my way to the other end of the restaurant where they had a wine bar and indulge in a nice glass of Pinot Noir. I sat alone and sipped my drink, though I could tell someone was watching me. Every time I turned around, I caught a glimpse of an attractive man, my age, who kept gazing in my direction. I finally decided that since he must think I was something to look at, I would be brave and bold and do the same to him!

I got out my compact from my purse, opened it up, and angled it just so. The next thing you know, he caught me looking at him in the mirror, and we both just started laughing. The next few hours flew by while we sat and talked at length about anything and everything. He had been divorced for a while, too, and was also simply just passing the time in the bar so he didn't have to go home alone. His kids were grown and out on their own.

We started dating, and as the weeks passed, we saw each other more and more. Now, I was quite careful not to introduce him to my daughter until I knew he would be a major part of my life. I also made it quite clear there would be no moving in together. We would either date indefinitely or get married. I was not going to put my child in a position of having her mother's boyfriend live with us because that is just simply not how I was raised, nor is it something I believe in. He was a little hesitant about that plan, but we decided to set a date to talk about the future. We chose to wait six months. At that point, we would go to dinner and decide. The months passed, and we fell more in love.

Now, I have to add things did progress a little faster for us than for most couples, and that is because he is a firefighter. That just naturally brings stronger emotions because when you watch the one you love run out the door all the time and you really never know if they will come back, it changes a part of you and makes you love that person even more and on a deeper level.

The time was approaching for the magical six-month talk where we would make adult decisions as to where we were really going to take the relationship. We made dinner reservations. I bought a new dress, set up a babysitter for my daughter, and thought I was ready to state my case to him that we either end things or plan a wedding. I really was sure I would be OK with either decision.

As fate would have it, there was a major fire that night, and he showed up late to dinner. He still had that telltale smell of a burning building, and it melted my heart.

I threw out everything I had planned to say and just looked at him and said, "I really do not want to be the last one called if something happens to you because I am just simply your girlfriend."

He said nothing. He looked down for what seemed to be forever and moved over to be closer to me. The next thing I knew, he was down on one knee, looking up at me. He still had some soot and ashes on his face.

He just said, "You're right, and I can't bear the thought of that. Will you marry me?"

In March of 2010, we were married at a small church adjacent to the firehouse, as that just seemed fitting, based on our story. We have had three years of love, compassion, and a real marriage that only comes when both people have that epiphany where they just know neither can be without the other.

#39 KENZIE AND JAKE

When we first got together, I was instantly crazy about him! I do not know if it was his beautiful brown eyes or the cute little dimples on both sides of his chubby cheeks. Either way, I was smitten. I wanted to spend every second with him. And that is what I did.

After just three months, we decided to move in together. Life made too much sense, and why pay for two places when we were always at mine? After a few months of living together, it occurred to me:

"This is exactly what I want life to be."

It was so exciting just thinking about it. So, one night after dinner I brought marriage up. Let's just say we weren't exactly on the same page.

Apparently, he was not "into getting married again."

I knew he had been married before, but he hadn't been even eighteen yet, and it had only lasted six months. How does that even count? I was so upset.

He knew it, too! He kept trying to make me feel better with reasons why just living together was just as good, if not better then being married. He'd say things such as:

"Its just a piece of paper."

"You would have to spend hours changing your name on everything."

167

"The stress of a wedding is enough to drive people to murder."

"The cost of a wedding could be a down payment on our house."

And, "You do not have to be married to do all of the things married couples do."

I spent the next few weeks really thinking about why marriage was so important to me and pondering his reasoning for not wanting to get married. One day, I was OK with not getting married, then the next it was a top priority. What little girl doesn't dream of getting married in a big white dress in front of hundreds of people? Finally, the little girl inside yelled out to me in my head, loud and clear:

"I want my wedding! I want him to marry me!"

A few days later, we were wandering through a department store looking for a blender so we could make milkshakes that night for game night. He had volunteered to buy it since he suggested milkshakes. When we got to the small appliances area, he about choked when he saw the price tags.

I told him, "I'll buy it."

He said, "It doesn't really matter, does it? We're in the same house."

Ha! This was my way in.

I quickly replied, "Sure, but if we break up, it's mine, and you will have to spend the money to buy one anyway."

He looked stunned for a second.

Before he could open his mouth to speak, I continued, "And if you buy it so that you can take it with you, it only leaves you $40 to last the next two weeks.

Whereas if we were married, it could come out of the household joint account, and your play money could be left alone."

"OK, OK, so getting married would make money matters a little easier. That is still not worth wasting the money on a wedding."

"Wasting, huh?" I picked up the purple blender and walked toward the cash register without saying another word.

We had a lot of fun that night, but I did not forget our conversation. After everyone was gone, the house was put back together, and he had gone to bed, I sat down to write a letter. I explained to him my personal beliefs on why marriage is so important, how I knew he was the one I wanted to spend the rest of my life with, but how I would not settle on just being roommates. My letter also included things such as:

"I don't think of the cost of a wedding as a waste. I think of it as an investment in our future. A little skin in the game always makes the commitment stronger." and

"The cost of a blender is worth the cost to see the character of a man." and

"A relationship is about compromise. We all do things we do not want to in order to make our spouse happy. Can't fill in the spouse line if there is no marriage."

I concluded with, "I am sorry, but if we aren't married, then I am just an option you choose for now. I don't want to be an option."

I left the letter leaned against the blender, and I left. I was not not sure how he would react. I did not know if my heart would end up shattering or if he would do what I wanted him to.

I did not sleep a wink that night. I hated sleeping alone, first of all, and I could not stop thinking about what was going to happen next. I replayed a hundred scenarios in my head over and over again. He did not call me the next day or the day after that. I was falling apart. I was hating myself. Why did I push him? Why couldn't I just leave well enough alone?

On the third day without him, I had to work. I pulled myself together and decided, "This is what I asked for."

When I walked into work that day, there was a vase with a dozen roses on my desk.

The note said:

"NOT AN OPTION."

I expected him to call or text or something. Nothing. As I was leaving work that night, confused on what to do, I wanted to call him! I wanted to hear his voice and tell him I was stupid. I could not let myself do that. Roses do not replace a lifelong commitment. When I got to my car that night, he was there.

He was in a tux. He got down on bended knee and proposed.

Later that night, I asked him, "What changed your mind? What part of my letter struck you?"

He shook his head and said, "The letter was beautiful, but waking up without you was like waking up without my right arm."

I guess it is all about finding the holes you fill for him. We were married on May 27, 2009.

#40 KATHI AND DAN

The truth is, when I met Dan I was not looking for a husband. Indeed, I had just ended a relationship with a man who was pushing for a more serious commitment. I was a fiercely independent woman, still trying to make it on my own. All that changed the night the two of us met at a local restaurant. We met in the summer of 2000 when I was 24 years old. I knew from the first conversation I had with Dan that I wanted to marry him. However, he was not so sure.

We had seen each other around a time or two before. He'd caught my eye at my friend Landry's 4th of July party the previous year, then again during a weekend at her lake house. I had inquired about his status, but she had told me that he was in a serious relationship. I have never been the type of person to pursue someone who is committed. Therefore, I put him out of my mind for good. He only knew me as "Landry's friend Kathi" and had never given me a second thought.

The night Landry invited a bunch of us out to meet her new husband was interesting. The newlyweds showed up late, which gave Dan and I a chance to talk for the first time. I learned that he and his long-term girlfriend had recently broken up after he had bought a $5,000 engagement ring for her but before he'd been able to offer it. He was devastated. He swore that he would never marry. I thought it was the grief talking, but I had no idea how pervasive that thought was in his mind.

I promised myself that night that we wouldn't get together right away. I wasn't interested in someone who was on the rebound, and I was certain that we would end up together eventually. I was very right. We were a serious couple by Christmas, and I was hearing wedding bells by New Year's. Dan, on the other hand, said that wedding bells were not in his future.

He said, "I want to be with you every night and day. Let's move in together."

I must have communicated something in the way I looked at him, because he rushed on.

"We could combine our finances, or keep them separate. It's all up to you. We would make all of the household decisions together. We could even talk about having children. I just, I don't want any part of a wedding."

"But..."

"I already made that decision—and it backfired on me."

I told Dan in no uncertain terms, "I will not bring children into the world without being married first."

I wasn't trying to coax him or play a trick on him in any way. I was completely honest. I wanted children, but I wanted them to feel the sense of unity and trust that comes from being in a family that is totally committed to one another. How could my children feel commitment when their father wasn't even willing to commit to their mother?

Still, Dan stood fast to his position. He reminded me, "When we first met, you weren't looking for a husband."

"I've changed, and I'm no longer satisfied with just dating."

This was a time that I had to make a decision. Did I stand up for myself and my future family? Or, did I give in and spend my (unwed) days with the man of my dreams? It wasn't a hard choice for me. I broke things off with Dan.

I told him, "If you can't commit to me, then we need to go our separate ways."

The time apart was good for us. It gave him time to reflect on how his decision to not marry would affect the rest of his life. It gave me the chance to look at the dating pool once more and realize that there truly was no one else for me.

Almost exactly one year from the time we had our first meal together, I went to Dan's office and asked him out for a friendly evening. He agreed. We met at the same restaurant where we had first spoken. I wanted to grab him, shake him, tell him to snap out of it and start wedding planning with me, but I knew better.

I kept my calm and told him, "I'm glad we can be friends."

Tears came to his eyes, but he just nodded.

We had pleasant conversation throughout the meal. At the end, he offered to walk me to my car. I told him no and I left on my own.

Dan called that evening.

We talked for hours about nothing and everything. We made plans for that weekend, but I reminded him it would be just as friends.

I could hear his sigh, but I knew I had to keep up the charade.

He needed to see exactly what he was missing out on by not proposing marriage.

This pattern continued for the rest of the summer. Yes, it was a long investment of time and energy, but it was well worth it. Dan was pledging his undying love to me by Labor Day.

He said, "I swear I'll consider marriage if you only consider giving me another chance."

I looked him right in the eye and said, "Single stone, round cut, platinum band."

We both chuckled, then laughed, then embraced.

My friends thought I was crazy to go back to someone who wasn't serious about me. I was almost 26 by this time, and many of them were already married. But, I felt the change within him. I could see in his eyes that he was serious about being serious.

Two weeks later, Dan took me for a drive. We were supposed to go out to dinner and a movie, but he said he just wanted to go talk someplace quiet. This was not out of character for him, so I thought very little of it. I was irritated that I wouldn't be seeing the movie, but I was mostly happy to be back with the love of my life.

I was never more surprised than when he turned onto a dirt road in the middle of nowhere and parked the car. He looked at me, smiled, then produced the box. The ring was gold with a square cut stone flanked by by two gems. He'd gotten the ring completely wrong, but somehow it was perfect.

We got married six months later, in 2002. After 12 years of marriage, I can honestly say that I love my husband and our two children more with every passing day. And Dan? He doesn't understand why anyone wouldn't want to be married.

#41 CINDY AND BOB

We met at a small private college. We actually met our Freshman year, but were just friends at first. Six months later, we knew we liked each other for more than just friends. We began dating in March, 1988. He was a business major, and I was a social work major. He was easy going, and I was stubborn.

He played baseball, and I was his biggest fan.

He was a talented pitcher, and he got invited to try out for a professional baseball team in Chicago. I will never forget the day of his tryout. He threw well, and the talent scouts clocked his throws at 92 miles per hour. They were interested in him signing up for the minor leagues. That could lead to the possibility of being recruited by the major leagues. I was excited. You can imagine my surprise when he said he wasn't planning on joining the minor leagues.

I asked why.

He said, "Who knows how long I would play in the minor leagues before I ever got to play in the major leagues?" He also said, "What I really want to do is to start a family with you."

I was over the moon!

And then the weird part came.

He wanted to move in together, have our kids, and not get married right away.

I was tempted to move in with him, but I declined. I knew what would happen if we lived together, and I didn't want to start a family without a commitment.

"Living together before marriage is like playing house," I told him. "I've seen too many couples who just lived together split up as soon as they had a difference of opinion."

He asked me, "How do I know if I can live with you if we don't at least try before we get married?"

I asked him, "How do you know you can't live without me? The only way to really get to know each other is to get married, then earn the privilege of living together."

He finally agreed just because he knew I was stubborn and was not going to waiver.

We hugged each other tight and told our families of our engagement.

"Besides," I told him, "I only want to belong to one person. If we get married first, then you'll be the only person I have ever been with."

He said, "Thank you for this reassurance that you'll never cheat."

Faithfulness was a good indication that we would stay together forever. We got married on June 15, 1991, in the afternoon at a small Lutheran church. It was an interesting day. The day started out raining, yet during our wedding the sun came out. It was almost as if God was shining down on our marriage vows. The church was full, and it was one of the happiest days of my life. I am happy to report that we have stayed married all these years. We also have two beautiful daughters. It has been a wonderful life.

#42 KIMBER AND HANK

First of all, I had been living with him for about a year before I decided that I wanted to get him to propose to me. Hank was the type of person who never wanted to get married, at least he was for the year that we were together as boyfriend/girlfriend, so I knew it would be a difficult task to get him to propose to me.

After I decided I wanted Hank to propose to me, I started to brainstorm, and it was hard figuring out what I should do first. I remember I picked up a magazine and there was a section that was quite comical but held some truth to it. The article was about how a woman refused to make love to her husband until he did something that she wanted him to do. Obviously, I wasn't going to tell Hank that if he didn't propose to me, we would stop making love. I was kind of sneaky about it. I slowly started to make love with Hank less and less.

Eventually, he asked me, "What's going on with us never making love anymore?"

I told him, "I've decided that I have a new goal, and that goal is to stop making love until I get married."

This was a major hint that I dropped to him, but I wanted him to think that I meant when I found a husband, not necessarily waiting on him to become my husband.

Hank was taken back and was speechless and even stopped talking to me for a few days.

It wasn't long before he said:

"I respect your decision, and I love you regardless if we make love or not."

When he said that, I figured it wouldn't be long.

A few weeks went by, and then he said, "I want to take you to visit New York City for the weekend."

I had no clue what was in store for me because once a month we usually go away for the weekend, and he usually chooses where we go.

When we arrived in NYC, it was a hot summer day, and on the last day we were there he brought me to the Empire State building. We went up to the observation deck.

After about five minutes, he gave me this big speech, "I care for you so much, Kimber. I never want to lose you..." He kept going on and on and on.

I was certain he was going to propose to me there and then, but he didn't. I was devastated and thought there was no way he was going to propose to me now. I could tell that he knew I thought that I was about to be proposed to.

However, a few days after we returned home, he proposed to me from out of the blue.

I woke up and started to make breakfast, and then he came up to me and got down on one knee and proposed to me. I was definitely taken back.

After he proposed to me, we had to set a date for the wedding. We decided to make the wedding date for February 14, 2000. He proposed to me on October 1, 1999, but the struggle still wasn't over.

He said he only had one objection about getting married, and that was he was afraid that once we got married he would have less time to do the things that he could do when he was not married. I didn't want him to think things would change, so I sat him down and we talked for a good hour. I explained to him that nothing would change, and I comforted him, and before I knew it he was completely fine with getting married.

A few months passed by, and before we knew it, 2000 came, and then February 14 came. I was very nervous, and so was he. We had the wedding on a beach in Hawaii. Now we have been married for more than 10 years, and not much has changed since we were just living together. He still gets to do what he wants, when he wants, and so do I. However, we are much happier now.

#43 MARIE AND TOMMY

My husband and I have been through a lot. Though we met through a mutual friend a few years before we started dating, there is a lot more to our story that the typical relationship. Our friend introduced us in early 2003, while I was still in high school for my senior year. Tommy had graduated the year before, but we hit it off right away. We both love music, camping, and having a good time.

We started to hang out quite a bit more, even went on a few trips together to another friend's cabin, but we never dated. In 2004, he started going out with another girl, and I began dating another guy, but we kept in contact the whole time. Tommy and I became really good friends. There was always an attraction, but we lived almost an hour and a half apart, so it didn't seem wise to begin a relationship.

As we got to know each other, we shared details about our pasts. He'd grown up in a family without a dad, and my mom was absent, so we had pretty similar experiences. When it came to relationships, he'd had more than me, and had gotten hurt a handful of times—not because of anything that he had done directly, but just because things did not work out.

He and I had a lot of serious conversations, hinting at dating each other, but we didn't really know how to make it work, even though we flirted quite a bit immediately upon meeting each other. Though we'd kept in contact, we hadn't talked as much as we probably should have.

And then in late 2005, something awful happened. The mutual friend who had introduced us died unexpectedly, leaving all of us to deal with a tragedy. Tommy and I reconnected. Although I was in college, we began spending more time together, which led to a relationship. There were a few times that we both joked about the death leading to at least one good thing, but it didn't seem real until we decided to move in together.

Things got serious fast. We lived together, traveled together, finished school together. He became a part of my family and I with his.

It was going really well until the subject of getting married came up. A lot of our friends were getting engaged and having kids, and with the way things were going for us, it seemed natural for us to follow, but Tommy's demeanor changed whenever the topic came up. I knew that he'd had some bad luck with girls in the past, but it hadn't seemed like such a big deal or anything that would have scared him away from a permanent commitment to someone that loved him as much as I do.

We went on a vacation to Florida in the summer of 2007, after I'd graduated college. It was really romantic. We were right on the beach, went to a few fancy dinners, had an amazing time... but something was up. He was acting strange. I confronted him the second to last night before we were to leave, asking why he seemed kind of off and why he didn't seem to be enjoying the trip. He shuffled around on the sand, wouldn't meet my eyes.

Finally, he said, "I'm acting weird because I really don't think I should ask you to marry me like everyone assumed I was going to while we were here."

I was in shock. Did that mean that he wanted to

marry me, or that he didn't anymore?

I told him, "We're going back to the hotel room and having a conversation about what you just told me."

And we did, but it wasn't what I was expecting.

Tommy told me, "I love you, and I want to be with you, but I want to be absolutely sure that we aren't together because our friend died and we feel as if we owe it to his memory. Yes, I seriously have considered marrying you and growing old together, but I want to do it with a clear conscience."

I was stunned, but relieved that his doubt wasn't coming from anything that I had said or done. I took a deep breath and spilled my heart out to him, tears and all.

I assured him, "Even though that may have been the reason we decided to try a relationship, it's not the one that's kept us together for almost three years. There's nothing I want more than to marry you, and even though I'm content to live with you and be in a relationship, I don't want to do that forever. I can't wait to make it 'official'."

Right in the middle of that conversation, the power in the hotel went out because of a thunderstorm, but I kept talking.

I explained to him, "Even though I'm not super experienced with long-term relationships, I know you make me happy. Even if you're worried that something bad is going to happen like it did with your other girlfriends, I know what it's like to grow up with only half a family. I don't want that for our kids."

Tommy was mostly silent, which scared me a little, but I didn't want to have to rehash the same conversation at another time, and I felt that it was important to get everything out at once.

My little tirade lasted almost five minutes after the power went out, and when I finally finished, he was still silent.

I asked him, "Do you understand?"

He quietly said, "Yeah, I guess."

That was it.

I was stunned. I didn't even know how to respond. Luckily, I didn't have to.

When the power came on, I was sitting in silence at the end of our bed, facing the small table that he had been sitting at, but Tommy was no longer on the chair. He was on one knee with a small box in his hands.

Eight months from that day—March 21, 2008—we were married, and neither of us has looked back. To this day, I believe that the conversation we had in our pitch black Floridian hotel room was the thing that made him decide to take the risk and ask me.

#44 TIMOTHY AND KELLY LOMAX

I had always dreamed of the perfect wedding, just like any other girl out there: beautiful flowers and all my bridesmaids dressed in blue. In my fairy tale, the church was full of smiles from family and friends with barely enough room to seat everyone. I had my vows written before I was ten and expected the same from my groom to be. Sometimes, our fairy tales are just that: stories that exist only in our minds, where everything is in perfect order and everyone lives happily ever after. Well, I am most certainly living my happily ever after, but that is the only part of my story that stayed the same.

In early 2004, I met my prince after years of searching all the wrong places for all the wrong men. Tim was tall, dark and handsome, just what I had dreamed of all those years, but he was so far out of my league. You know what I mean: way more good looking and popular than me. I didn't know how I could even open my mouth to say "Hello" to him, let alone start up a conversation.

In the smoke filled, noisy piece of a pub we were at, I spent what felt like hours just getting up the courage to make eye contact with this amazing man. We finally made eye contact by accident when I was looking at the chalkboard menu behind the bar and he walked in front of me. At least, I think it was by accident. Before I shyly looked away, I saw his sweet, inviting smile. Tim walked right up to me and whispered in my ear.

"What's your name?"

I cleared my throat and tried to stop my heart from beating out of my chest.

I said, "My name is Kelly," and smiled sweetly, though I knew my face must be flushed due to the massive panic attack I was trying desperately to control without it being noticed.

He bought two drinks, and we sat together and watched people dance without much conversation that first night.

I was just so amazed that this awesome guy was sitting with me! There were a lot of very pretty girls there that night, so I wondered why he chose me. Needless to say, I broke my number-one bar rule that night: never ever give out your correct phone number. I was hoping he would call but knew in my mind that I was kidding myself. Mine must have been one of many numbers he collected that night, right?

Much to my surprise, my phone rang around noon the next day.

It was Tim, saying, "Can I come see you?"

I couldn't say, "No." After all, I had given him the right number.

We were together every day for a few years after that. For the first year, I patiently waited on that magic question. After that, I started to fear we would never marry and make my fairy tale come true. Once a month or so, I would drop a hint, but in those early times he didn't take them well.

Tim had so many doubts about getting married, you know, the whole "If it ain't broke, don't fix it" mentality. He had been through a lot coming from a broken home as a child, and he was terrified that he would end up hurting his own children if we ever got divorced.

As the months and then years went by, I felt more and more like something was missing from my life. I felt like I had put in enough time with him to carry his last name.

Still reluctant after about two and a half years, he decided that we could at least entertain the conversation of marriage. It was a short conversation, but it was promising just the same.

He said, "Why do you want to get married so bad?"

I told him, "I want to spend the rest of my life with you. I want to start a family and plan our future together."

He smiled at me. "I want those things, too."

I began to think that just maybe there was a chance, after all. He had never initiated the conversation of marrying me before that moment, so I guess I knew deep down that we were getting closer to being Mr. and Mrs. Timothy Lomax. I had always loved his last name; it was such a strong and bold last name. I wanted to share it.

In late 2006, I was working full time as a sales manager, and Timothy was the credit manager in the store across the street. We'd been working across the street from each other for about a year, and every day we took lunch together.

He still had his doubts about getting married, but by this point in our relationship he was making promises of one day making my dream come true. I was finally thinking of that beautiful white dress again, and even at the age of 28 I still wanted my bridesmaids wearing blue. I had even searched the Internet for caterers and looked at a ton of cakes. I kind of felt like that little girl again, only now I knew what my groom looked like.

We made it through the Christmas holidays and still no engagement ring. I was a little disappointed, but I didn't let him know that. Life went on as normal. As New Year's approached, I looked forward to it this year more than any because I just knew that my prince would pop the question. Well, New Year's came and went, and I had all but given up on becoming Mrs. Kelly Lomax.

Just when I was feeling my lowest about the whole situation, something life changing happened to me out of the blue.

On February 21, 2007, Tim came to pick me up for lunch as he always did. We were both starving and each dressed in our work uniforms. Little did I know, we were not going to eat lunch. We pulled up at the court house, and my family was there waiting on us. Tim took me as his wife that day on a one-hour lunch break in the county courthouse in our work clothes.

I asked him that night, "What changed your mind about making me your wife?"

He said, "I couldn't imagine spending the rest of my life with my girlfriend. I want to spend it with my wife."

Even though I didn't get the wedding of my dreams that day, he made me feel like the most special girl in the world. I will never ever forget my wedding day, the day I got his last name. We have been married for 6 years now, and every moment with him is just as special as that day. We now have three beautiful children and are truly living happily ever after.

#45 SARAH AND ANDREW

During my second year at university, I happened to get a chance to interact with Andrew for the first time. The interaction was more of a coincidence in itself. Our world history teacher had sorted us by count for a group assignment and its presentation. When the sorting was done, somehow everybody except Andrew had at least one partner. My own group consisted of three other girls and me. Our teacher, looking at Andrew's condition, made a change in our grouping, a change that was going to alter the entire course of my life! I still don't know what made Mr. Matthews change his mind and shift my group, but I was left to partner with Andrew alone. I didn't know the guy, hadn't ever talked to him, and he looked so rude!

How did Mr. Matthews imagine I would be able to work with Rude Boy in harmony and get the project completed on time? I opposed the change, but Mr. Matthews made me be quiet and threatened me with a loss in marks. I had no choice but to reluctantly partner with Andrew. I had to shift next to him during the class that day. The entire lesson, I kept cursing Andrew and Mr. Matthews in my heart. At the end of the class, I got up and rushed outside. I didn't want to face anyone that very moment, not when I was seething with anger at the unfair change I had to go through in my grouping.

I was waiting outside for my friends when along came Andrew.

"Can I talk to you for a moment?"

"Yes," I said reluctantly. What else could I do?

In the sexiest male voice I had ever heard, spoke Andrew, "I'm very sorry you had to go through this trouble because of me. If you could just wait a minute and accompany me to Mr. Matthews's study, I might be able to persuade him to let you off the hook. I'll manage on my own."

What could I say? I was mesmerized the moment he opened his mouth. Nothing he said registered with me, and I nodded my head like a fool. Soon, Mr. Matthews came out, and we followed him to his study.

"I'm sorry to disturb you, Mr. Matthews, but I just wanted to say: if you could let Sarah off the hook, I'll manage my project on my own."

"I'm afraid I can't do that now, Andrew. It's final now. Sarah is going to partner you in the project, or else she loses marks."

I gulped audibly. Why was Mr. Matthews being so stubborn? What had I done to deserve this?

I curtly choked out a "Thank you," and left the study without even a backward glance.

Outside, Andrew stopped me. "I'm sorry."

"It's OK."

"I suppose we'd best have a way to reach each other."

"Yeah, I guess."

We exchanged contact numbers and headed off our separate ways. That night, on 8th March 1993, Andrew called me for the first time, to discuss the project. I don't know what it was about us, but we instantly clicked. Ideas for the project came pouring out, and before we knew, we had been on the phone for more than an hour, and neither one of us seemed eager to hang up. We both were bright, and it took us just two weeks to wind up the entire assignment. But, what had started as a totally assignment based contact had changed.

In the two weeks that had passed, Andrew and I had become addicted to each other. We could talk all day and not get tired. And then on the last day of the semester, I realized I was in love with him! I was naïve enough to rush up to him and exclaim in a rush:

"I love you! I want to spend my entire life with you!"

He stood there for a moment with his mouth open, not saying anything, but to my infinite delight, confessed, "I love you, too."

Our relation progressed, but we played it low for three solid years. I had my ideas of keeping it low till marriage, while Andrew was totally opposed to being married. His parents's marriage had failed, and it had spoiled the love bond they shared, destroying the image of the marital institution in Andrew's mind. He was ready to live with me, and asked me to move in with him. He didn't mention marriage, and I knew that wasn't something he had in mind.

I felt let down. I had planned my entire future with the guy, and he wasn't ready to give me a commitment. The day he said no to my idea of getting married before moving in together, I was totally broken and cried myself to sleep. After spending three years in a relationship with me, he had doubts about our compatibility as husband and wife. I decided to talk to Andrew straight and get a final answer.

It was the 9th of December, 1997 when I confronted Andrew with a determination.

191

"Andrew, I really want us to be married."

"Marriage is awful; I've seen it. You know that."

"I love you more than anything in this world, Andrew, and I will never let it be awful between us, but if we can't be married, then I will have to leave you."

Because I had made him clear it was all or nothing this time, I knew he would cave in to my threat because he loved me so much, and that's what exactly happened. On that beautiful evening of 9th December 1997, Andrew and I promised to tie the knot come next spring.

It was 16th April, 1998 when I walked down the aisle towards Andrew. Our love was a strong bond that had survived and killed all his oppositions. I knew I had threatened him into this marriage, but the smile that dawned on his face when he saw me walking towards him as his bride was enough to convince me that he was taking the step with all his heart.

#46 JAIME AND JOEL

We had been dating for two years, and Joel still hadn't met my dad. I was scared for Joel to meet him. I had never introduced a man to Dad, and I knew that when the day came, that better be the one I married. I was not going to risk giving Dad a heart attack knowing that his baby girl had a man in her life unless I knew he was worth it. Well, two years had come, and Joel said, "I can't take our relationship seriously if I don't know your whole family." I got worried and told my mom what Joel had said. She suggested bringing Joel to dinner, so I called Dad to ask his permission.

He was hesitant at first, and said, "Let me think about it."

I got off the phone, wondering what Dad could possibly have to think about.

Dad called Mom to ask questions about this Joel character. Mom told me all about it later.

"Do you know this young man? Is he the sort our daughter should be spending her time with? Do we know who his parents are? Are they good people?"

Mom assured Dad that Joel's family were good people, worthy of their daughter.

When Dad got home from work, I asked, "Have you come to a decision?"

"Well, Baby Girl, I suppose we can give this Joel a

chance. Yes, you may invite him out to dinner with us this coming Friday at Max's. I'm paying."

I was so excited! I called Joel and said, "You got your wish. You're invited out to dinner this Friday with my whole family, starting at six. Meet us at Max's. Don't be late!"

After a long and anxious week, it was finally Friday. Joel had kept calling all week, asking me:

"What should I wear?"

"Should I hide my tattoos?"

"What does your mom want for her birthday?"

I told him it was a good idea to hide the tattoos. I didn't want to spring that on Dad at the first meeting. Joel showed up to the restaurant with a bag from Godiva. He knew how to make Mom happy, but would he survive Dad?

Joel came up to our table and shook Dad's hand.

It was so awkward. I wasn't sure if I should kiss him, hug him, or even touch him. He definitely wasn't trying to touch me in Dad's view! I ended up just smiling my best smile at Joel, and then blushing all through dinner whenever his arm brushed against mine as we ate side by side.

Dinner went well. Joel was extremely quiet and only spoke when he was asked a question.

Dad asked, "What do you do, Son, and where are you from?"

Joel said, "I'm enlisted, in the Navy. So was my father, so I grew up in multiple places, one being Stockton."

Dad had also grown up in Stockton. Once Dad heard Stockton, he seemed to stop asking questions.

I wasn't sure if that was good or bad.

Dinner ended, and I asked, "Joel, would you give me a ride home, please?"

I wanted to give Mom a chance to ask Dad what he thought.

In the car, Joel said, "I think it went well. Do you?"

"Did you notice the questions stopped after your Stockton answer?"

Joel replied, "Your dad's from there. He knows how we Stockton people are."

Once I got home, Mom said, "The ride home was pretty quiet until your dad said, 'He seems like a nice kid.'"

I said, "I guess that's better than 'I don't ever want Jaime to see that boy again!'"

After that first dinner, Dad always said to invite Joel.

For the next year, Joel came over and remained quiet and respectful. By our three year mark, Joel was leaving for another deployment. As that time got close, we had The Talk.

I said, "I'm not sure if I can wait for you any longer without a proposal. I feel like we're getting nowhere."

Joel got a big grin on his face. He said, "That's what I needed to hear. I want to marry you, too! Let's do this the right way."

"What do you mean?"

He said, "Well, first, I don't want to surprise you with a ring because you're the one who has to wear it. I want you to pick it out with me. Second, I respect your dad, and I want to ask for his permission."

Hearing Joel say that made me know even more that he was the right man. I had finally found someone who not only respected and loved me but my family as well.

The next two months we spent shopping for a ring. I told him my requirements in size, setting, color, and karat. I had educated Joel on shopping for the perfect diamond so that he paid more attention to details that I had never noticed. He got my ring custom-made and was ready to ask Dad.

Joel came to our regular Sunday barbecue.

Dinner was over, Joel did his normal routine, sat quietly. Mom and I waited for two hours, and Joel still hadn't made his move.

I asked Joel, "Are you going to do it?"

He said, "I'm scared."

Dad was watching TV.

When a commercial break came on, Joel finally made his move.

"Sir, can I talk to you?"

As soon as I heard that, I left the room. Joel was sweating. Mom and I listened through the closed kitchen door.

"I love your daughter very much, Sir. I want to provide for her and take care of her for the rest of my life."

Dad gave Joel a lecture, "Well now, Son, she is my baby. She has expensive taste, and she can be difficult to deal with, but she needs your patience, love, and understanding."

"I hear you, Sir. You're right about that."

Dad said, "Well, as long as you know what you're getting into, you have my permission."

With that, Joel said, "Do you mind if I get something from my car?"

"You go right ahead, Son."

Joel ran to the car to get the ring. He got one one knee, still sweating, and said:

"Jaime, I love you and want to be with you for the rest of our lives. Will you marry me?"

Me being the smarty that I am, and wanting to make Joel sweat even more, I said, "Well, I have to think about it," and then I couldn't let him suffer even another second. I threw my arms around Joel and said, "Of course I will!"

Dad was so happy for us, he had us posing for pictures on his smart phone.

One year later, we were married In Las Vegas on May 15, 2012.

#47 LOIS AND JEFFREY

How did I convince him to marry me and not just remain living partners forever? Well, it is a simple but very complex story. Only complex because it took years upon years for our minds to click on this one simple idea. Alright, here is how I did it.

The main reason why he never proposed to me was due to financial constraint. In other words, as I was learning years later, he told me that because he was not making enough money, he decided he could not propose to me.

However, it all started back on the night we met. It was love at first sight. Jeffrey and I became attached to each other and could not spend a day apart. After nine months, we moved in together, and things were going great. We both had full time jobs. I am a practicing nurse, and he was a sales associate for a small company. We made ample time to be together despite our hectic schedules. We attended church every Sunday and were leading a good life. Many more weeks passed. Weeks turned into months, and months turned into years.

After five years, I started to wonder and worry.

"Why aren't we engaged yet?"

"How come he hasn't proposed to me?"

"Is it something I'm doing?"

However, as upset as I was, and curious, I still did not have the courage to face my fears and have a discussion with him. I was afraid, and wouldn't you be, too? To be confrontational about such a sensitive subject I thought would be too much.

After another year, I started to doubt myself and my own ideas of what was right and normal. I was thinking, "Maybe we don't need marriage. Perhaps, since this is the 21st Century, we don't need to get married."

Truth be told, I felt married, as we were quite a committed couple. But friends and family members started to ask uncomfortable questions. The subject of children came up at dinners with friends, and there was a lot of commotion amongst our co-workers as well as our closest friends as to what the situation between us was. To me, Jeff was more than my boyfriend, more than my companion, and certainly more than my partner in life. He felt like my husband, and I felt like his wife. But the questions still penetrated my mind and lingered there:

"Why aren't we married yet?"

"What is stopping him from asking me in marriage?"

These were just a few of the recurring thoughts and questions that went through my mind all those years.

This is what I did to finally get him to marry me:

I finally gave up my stubbornness and fear and told him that I was unhappy and might be falling into depression. I also explained to him that something had to change in our relationship, or it could not go on.

He was really struck by what I said, and a few weeks later he got a better job, for an insurance company downtown. He was making a significant amount more in salary each year. I was still a practicing nurse, and nothing changed on my end. We kept attending church regularly and made more time to be with each other despite our rigorous work schedules.

One beautiful fall day, Jeff told me we were going to Mexico for a winter vacation and to ask for my holiday time off in advance. So, I did, obviously, and I was eagerly awaiting this amazing vacation. Little did I know what was to come, but I was completely transfixed on this future occasion. It occupied my thoughts and my mind all the time. It was the first thing I could think about at work each day and the last I could dream about at night. I was merely dreaming of this vacation because in all nine years of our relationship we had never once been on a long vacation.

So, December rolled around, and our Mexico trip was just days away. Then, the day came, and we took off for Mexico. The weather was grand, the ocean was warm, and we were having the time of our lives.

Then, at dinner the waiter brought over the menus.

I opened mine, and out of the unusually large menu came a small square box.

My heart dropped.

Jeffrey stared at me with eyes that almost read, "go ahead, open it."

I did, and to my bright surprise the most beautiful diamond ring was inside.

Jeff stood up, took my hand, and asked me to marriage.

Of course, my answer was a glowing and ebullient "Yes!"

The rest of that trip was the best for me. We have been married for a few years now and been together for over a decade.

However, one day Jeff admitted to me why he never proposed all those years.

He said, "Honey, to tell you the truth, it wasn't until you asked me if I found a better paying job, if that would make me happier, that I realized I couldn't marry you unless I could support us entirely by my salary alone. I know this may sound foolish to you, but it is the truth. I needed to do this for myself and to plan our life together. Our security meant the world to me."

It's kind of funny relaying that message now, and even as I write it to you, I feel a strange pain in my heart. I never knew he was that concerned about monetary security. I thought we had a good life, strong love and were living happily on both our incomes. However, my husband is very traditional in many ways.

If I only knew then what I know now, I wonder, yes, I truly wonder if I would have whispered something into his ear to inspire him to marry me sooner than find another job. But, it all worked out for the best, and we have been enjoying our happiness ever since.

#48 JACK AND JOY O'REILLY

Jack and I have a passion for community theatre. That's how we met, back in 1997. We were doing the musical *Oklahoma!* with our local group of thespians. He played Curly, and I was a lowly chorus girl. I was 25 years old, but the director had cast me with the teenagers. I was one of those people who just looked younger. Jack jokes now that he stayed away from me because he thought I was "jail bait." I thought he was just an arrogant snob! Three years later, we were pronounced husband and wife: Mr. and Mrs. Jack and Joy O'Reilly.

I've always loved the way theatre people become so close and supportive of one another, like a family. Throughout the production, everyone in our cast of forty shared so much. We each did our parts, sometimes working long nights, and devoting our weekends. We ate together and got to know each other's very understanding families. We had parties at each other's homes. We laughed together, and sometimes, exhausted, we fought together, just like any typical family.

One night during that musical production, Jack was really getting on my nerves. We'd been working together for a month. He was always the life of the party, keeping everyone's spirits up with his good humor. Well, almost everyone's. He seemed to make a point of ignoring me, except to ask me to run little errands for him! He wasn't my boss or anything. Finally, I'd had enough.

In front of everyone, I blew up and told him, "I

do not tolerate disrespect from anyone, and I don't know what your problem is, or why you don't like me, but it is definitely your problem and not mine!"

When I get upset, I tend to cry, and to my horror, I felt the familiar heat rising in my face and the sting of tears, so I made a quick exit, leaving a very stunned cast in my wake.

That was a real turning point.

Jack apologized to me at the next rehearsal:

"I was really concerned after you peeled out of the parking lot, and I started asking around about you. Joy, I thought you were a kid! You're ten years older than I thought! Can I say that I would really like to take you out, not on a date, but to buy you dinner as an apology?"

By the end of the night, it was a date.

That date led to another date... and another.

Over the next three years, Jack and I became inseparable. He was a single dad of two adorable, precocious little girls. I was completely smitten with the way his eyes lit up when he talked about them. I knew he was a very loving father. As endearing as this was, it almost kept us from getting married.

Kali and Kelly were four and six when Jack and I started dating. Jack and their mom, Willow, had been high school sweethearts. They had gotten married while they were high school seniors. Jack told me that over the years Willow became more and more unhappy with married life. He'd thought their broken marriage could be mended with the birth of Kelly, but Willow seemed to sink deeper into depression, taking her anger out on him. She blamed him for everything and told him she had never wanted to be a mother, that she felt trapped. Jack took over all parental responsibilities, becoming both mother and father to little

Kelly.

When she became pregnant with Kali, Willow told Jack she planned to get an abortion.

Jack begged her to keep the baby. He promised if she would do that, he would free her from the marriage and raise the children on his own.

Willow agreed, and a month after Kali was born, she left.

Jack was heartbroken. He never heard from Willow again, but six months later a relative told him Willow had passed away, the result of a lethal combination of drugs and alcohol.

Jack used his love of theatre as an outlet. He said he loved that we shared the same passion.

"I don't want to lose you," he'd say, "but I don't trust that any relationship can last forever."

He had seen how feelings and relationships could change for the worse, and how the covenant of marriage had made Willow feel smothered and resentful. He never wanted to get mired down in such a destructive relationship again, and he absolutely did not want that to be any part of his children's lives. If their own mother would abandon them, what would happen to Kelly and Kali should our marriage go south? It was a chance he wasn't willing to take, no matter how much he loved me.

"Really? REALLY!" I all but shouted.

Obviously, this was not the acceptance Jack was seeking, but he listened, in stunned silence.

"So," I ranted, fighting back the inevitable tears, "you would deny your children the love and guidance of a woman who loves them every bit as much as she loves their father? You would deny them the chance at a real family... because you're afraid I might walk away! Well, let me tell you something, Bud, if you don't RESPECT me enough to make a real commitment to me, then you are DRIVING me away! Willow obviously had emotional issues" I went on. "Do I strike you as someone who is unstable?"

He looked at me as if that was just what he thought in that moment, but he had the good sense not to say so.

I told him sarcastically, "Oh, you're setting a fine example, living in fear of really loving, denying them the family they deserve!"

He made as if to speak, but I stopped him with my hand. I could feel the tears coming, and I had more to say.

"Mostly," I informed him, "you are setting them up to follow your example, possibly ruining their chances for a stable future, by not showing them what that looks like! Don't you want to walk your daughters down the aisle some day?"

What could he say to that? Nothing but:

"You're right. Joy, will you marry me?"

So, August 10, 2000, on an Ozark mountain hilltop near our own Arkansas home, two little girls beamed precociously bright smiles as they witnessed the beginning of our new, happily ever after family. At the reception, the D.J. played selections from *Oklahoma!* as our family and forty or so of our closest friends celebrated our joyous union.

#49 ANGELINE AND TOBY

I met Toby when I was 19. He had deep brown eyes and a striking appearance. He was also 13 years my senior. He was the sweetest man that I'd ever met, and he quickly became my best friend. I knew right away that he was the man I was supposed to marry. I fell in love. Toby was kind, smart, even tempered, and we shared the same spiritual beliefs—everything that I wanted in a mate. The first time he told me that he loved me, my heart melted. I was so happy with him, and it felt like we were destined to be together.

There was one problem, though. After a couple of fun-filled years of dating, our relationship seemed to be at a standstill. No matter how much I saw him, it didn't feel like enough. I wanted more. He appeared to have a phobia of commitment.

Toby was in his mid 30's and lived with his mother, as he had always done—minus the time he had spent away at college. His mother was a widow and disabled, so he claimed that he could not leave her. He was guilt ridden and consumed with the feeling of responsibility. Being an only child, he had a strong bond with his mother, leaving me afraid that it would be impossible for a wife to enter the picture.

He would tell me, "I love you …"

However, I could feel the pause on the end where he was leaving off, "but I can't marry you."

I kept trying to figure out what his issue was. Why was he holding back?

He told me, "Mother needs me. I'm all she has."

He is deeply religious, and strongly believes men should take care of their parents, especially widowed mothers.

I was touched that he cared for his mother.

Some people say, "How a man treats his mother, that's how he will treat his wife."

I admired him, but was also extremely hurt. The situation with his mother would not change—unless he was planning on putting his life on hold until she died. This was a very rough and emotional period for me. I grew weary of the relationship, yearning for much more. Every time I broached the subject of our future with him, he'd get uncomfortable and announce:

"Oh, look at the time. I gotta go."

I was left alone with my despair because he conveniently didn't want to talk about it.

I continued dating him, and my friends all thought I was silly and should move on to someone who would give me the future that I wanted. I attempted a few times to take a break from this relationship and see other men. Each time I started seeing someone different, he turned out to be a complete dud. I had already met my ideal mate, so I think that subconsciously I chose the wrong men to go out with. I kept ending up back with Toby. I was caught in a vicious circle that I eventually realized needed to stop.

I explained to him, "This can't continue. You are going to have to make a choice."

I was greatly scared.

I didn't think I would win.

How do you make a man choose between his mom and a wife?

I didn't even know if his mother was the true reason that he felt he couldn't get married. I honestly think that was only part of a greater issue, which I still don't fully understand.

Anyhow, I did win.

He pulled out a beautiful diamond ring and asked me to marry him. It was hard to believe we would actually be getting married. Eight years after we met, we were finally married in 2001. It was one of the happiest days of our lives.

Today, we have two wonderful sons. His mother lives about a mile away, by herself, and is doing fine. He now sees that the world did not come crashing down because he left his mom and started his own life. We do her grocery shopping, and she gets deliveries from Meals on Wheels because she has a very difficult time getting around. I still sense a little animosity because I "stole" her son, but generally our life is one with a happy ending—it just was a long wait, and I needed some patience.

#50 BARBARA AND JOHN

I had taken steps in my early life to be a good catch. That's very important when trying to seek companionship: be the sort of woman a man would want to spend the rest of his life with. I didn't do anything specifically to try to be a better catch, but all of the things I did were improvements over what those bar-girls were doing with their time. I always tried to make me all that I could be.

I was no athlete, but I did have a slim size 6 body when I met John. I worked out. I worked out a lot.

I learned a useful skill: I could already cook when I met him. Have you heard the saying, "The way to a man's heart is through his stomach"? Try cooking a man a good meal once a week or so. You might be surprised how well this works.

Also, my literature bachelor's degree was probably not as threatening to a man as a degree in, say, law, medicine, or accounting might have been.

That being said, I was also able to report some income every year since I turned thirteen. I never avoided hard work, and in fact relished some degree of challenge in the work place. I cannot say that I was a high-earner, but it was obvious from my work history that I would always try to help with the bills.

Furthermore, I had an incredibly good credit rating. I was not in debt, either. I got a co-signer for my first credit card when I wasn't even 18 yet, and that set me up for awesome credit later in life—because I never paid my bill late. I once was given a loan on a car based on a minimum wage job that I'd had for only three weeks. That's a great credit rating. I kept my student loan in the bank in college and repaid it one year after graduation. I worked part-time all through college, paid as I went, and had no need for a massive debt that would have followed me into adulthood.

Like I said, I wasn't one of those bar girls. After college, I worked full time and spent my spare time with friends who shared my hobbies and interests. My friends and I joined a hiking club that had outings where we met lots of people. We took fun art classes at the community college and went to museums.

More than anything else, remember that if you want to settle down and have a family, you won't get there by substance abusing, otherwise known as drinking and doing drugs. Guys might like to have a good time with someone who overdoes it, but they can't picture that woman caring for children. What's more, a man will avoid like the plague any invitation for you to meet his family if all you ever do is party (or if you dress like a tramp).

Besides, do you want the father of your children to be a drunk or an addict? No!

My point is:

There is more to be gained from becoming a good catch than there is from hanging out in bars or chat rooms. You don't have to be in those places to meet men.

You meet prospective mates every day: on trains and buses, through clubs you join and classes you take, at the grocery store, the park, the library, at work, at church, through friends and family... Don't sit at home all the time, but don't go places where all people are doing is drinking and doing drugs.

What matters is that when he meets us, we seem like "the one."

When he realizes that, then there is just something that clicks. He won't want to just live together if you are the best that you can be: sober, in shape, wearing something pretty, and living up to your potential.

If you're "the one," then he'll want to exchange rings and get something on paper before you get away!

If you have managed your money well, then the paperwork won't include a prenuptial agreement, either. He'll want to avoid that if your financial health is acceptable.

I guess I'd have to say that the best route to a good marriage is to invest heavily in becoming the person that you want to be first. Be tough if you want to meet a tough guy. Be a hero if you want to meet a hero. Be well educated if you want to spend your life with someone who is well educated. Develop career and financial goals if you want to attract someone who has the same goals. If you want to be married to a great-looking guy, then pay more attention to your own appearance.

John and I were married in 1993, after a very short courtship, but John and I were made for each other. Waiting for marriage before intimacy is easier when the courtship is a quick one. A short engagement is the best way to accomplish that one.

Lots of people today would just live together, but that wasn't enough of a commitment for me. Getting John to agree to marriage over living together was easy. All I did was beat him to the question. It was my idea, so his only choice was answering with either a simple "yes" or "no".

His only reservation was, "I intend to stay married

for life. I don't want any short timers."

I told him, "I don't see any point in divorce, since people always seem to remarry the same kind of person."

The most romantic part of our courtship was when he actually let me start to buy his clothes and influence his wardrobe choices. This is the kind of thing that doesn't last as long as the marriage does, yet it represents a high degree of trust when it does happen. With one fell swoop, I cleared out everything that he had left in his closets from high school. We went to a local department store, and he never looked back. This wasn't a complete make-over, but folks who had known him his whole life realized that he was changing.

Those who knew him before saw him mature very quickly and were surprised by that. He became career oriented rather than seeing work as a means to an end. He became more sociable when he had been something of a lone-wolf type before.

The biggest change came after were were married, when John became a family man. Occasionally, he voiced regret over driving a mini-van over a sports car. He even admitted missing his participation in sports so that he could take the kids to kid-friendly entertainment. But John grew as a man, and his childhood friends could see that responsibility was good for him.

How did marriage change me, you might be wondering?

I was never lonely again. Marriage gives you a permanent best friend. By the time we had two children, a hound dog, and an aloof cat join the household, there was never a dull moment. Once you have a family, there is scarcely any downtime, either. A family is an awful lot of work when a couple takes their responsibilities seriously:

helping with homework, counseling kids to make good choices for themselves, and supervising them or making sure they are supervised.

Eventually, those kids reach high school graduation, and the hound is both housebroken and has stopped teething. Money is more abundant, and good jobs seem easier to find. It would seem like time to sigh in relief, but no. That's usually when life throws you a curve that will knock the wind right out of you. It can be anything: a wayward adult child, cancer, or the loss of one or both of your jobs.

What is the glue that holds husband and wife together during tough times?

That's easy.

We have a good solid foundation in place from earlier years. Together, we developed our talents, and our opportunities grew in direct proportion to that effort. We have so many shared memories that really we seem like one person, rather than two. We know from millions of experiences over twenty years of marriage that we can trust each other, through thick and thin.

A solid foundation of experience and trust is the best defense against the vicissitudes of time.

THANK YOU

Thank you for reading this book.

I hope you will post a customer review to this book's page at Amazon.com. Customer reviews are a big way people discover new books these days.

If you wish to be in touch with me or to find out more about me, then please check out my weight-loss blog: Size 12 By St Patrick's Day.

I am writing novels based on some of these 50 true Marry Me stories. Be notified when these novels come out! Sign up here:

http://eepurl.com/w96_v

or, scan this QR code!

Best Wishes,

Cherise Kelley